Contents

Plan of book

	Topics/ Functions	Listening Skills	Grammar/ Vocabulary
Before you begin: How do you learn English?	Explaining types of listening	Listening for gist Listening for specific information Understanding inferences	
Unit 1: Getting to know you	Meeting people	Understanding questions Following instructions Identifying relationships	*Wh*-questions (present) Imperatives
Unit 2: What's your number?	Asking for and giving (numerical) information	Understanding and processing numbers	Numbers
Unit 3: I'm hungry!	Explaining how to make a food	Following instructions Identifying a sequence	Imperatives Sequence markers
Unit 4: Gestures	Describing gestures in different countries	Understanding cultural information Understanding cultural differences	Parts of the body Verbs of motion
Unit 5: Didn't you see that sign?	Stating rules and giving permission	Inferring meaning of signs Understanding rules	Modals: *can* and *should*
Unit 6: How do you feel?	Discussing health and habits	Identifying behavior Understanding suggestions	Simple present Imperatives
Unit 7: Where is it?	Asking for and giving directions	Identifying locations Following directions	Imperatives Prepositions of location
Unit 8: The world market	Discussing exports	Identifying origin Following directions	Adjectives of nationality Prepositions of location Modal: *should*
Unit 9: What do they look like?	Describing how people have changed	Understanding physical descriptions Identifying differences	Descriptive adjectives (people)
Unit 10: What do you do?	Talking about careers and future plans	Identifying occupations Understanding plans Inferring whether a situation is certain	Future with *going to* Future with *will*

	Topics/ Functions	Listening Skills	Grammar/ Vocabulary
Unit 11: **What are they** **talking about?**	Evaluating whether a topic of conversation is appropriate	Inferring topics Understanding relationships	Question forms (simple present)
Unit 12: **How was your** **vacation?**	Describing past activities	Understanding past activities Understanding emotions Following a story	Simple past tense
Unit 13: **Around the house**	Talking about household jobs and chores	Identifying attitudes Identifying preferences	Gerunds (-*ing* forms) Infinitives
Unit 14: **Shopping**	Talking about shopping for clothes and household items	Understanding descriptions Inferring decisions	Existential *to be* Descriptive adjectives (things)
Unit 15: **Going places**	Talking about and comparing countries	Identifying places Understanding questions and answers	Comparatives
Unit 16: **Making plans**	Making and changing plans	Identifying times and places	Future with *will* Future with *going to*
Unit 17: **Youth culture**	Discussing the interests of young people, past and present	Identifying mistakes Understanding details	Past tenses: simple past and past progressive
Unit 18: **Making a** **difference**	Discussing environmental issues	Understanding explanations Understanding details	Simple present Infinitive of purpose (*You use it to...*)
Unit 19: **It's in the news.**	Discussing current events	Inferring topics Understanding details	Past tenses: simple past and past progressive
Unit 20: **Dreams and** **screams**	Telling an unusual story	Understanding details Understanding and enjoying a story	Past tenses: simple past and past progressive Sequence markers

Acknowledgments

Culture Corner sources

43   *Book of Lists 3*, by A. Wallace, D. Wallaenchinsky, and I. Wallace. Corgi, 1984.

Illustrations

Adventure House   26, 48/49, 66/67
Daisy de Puthod   4 *(bottom)*, 11, 12, 14, 27/28, 47, 53, 58, 63, 70
Randy Jones   20, 25, 35, 41, 65
McNally Graphic Design   13, 29, 56, 68/69
Wally Neibart   15, 23, 30, 38, 40, 44, 46, 51, 57
Andrew Toos   3, 4 *(top)*, 5, 16, 17, 22, 33, 39, 42, 43, 50, 61
Sam Viviano   8, 32, 34, 36/37, 64

Photographic credits

The authors and publishers are grateful for permission to reproduce the following photographs.

6   *(from left to right)* © H. Gans/The Image Works; © Roy Bishop/Stock Boston; © Larry Dale Gordon/The Image Bank; © Walter Bibikow/The Image Bank
7   *(from left to right)* Rivera Collection/Superstock Inc.; © Hugh Rogers/Monkmeyer Press; © Frank Siteman/Stock Boston
26   Gamma Liaison
31   *(from left to right)* © Nancy Brown/The Image Bank; © P. Cantor/Superstock Inc.
45   © Richard Laird/FPG International
54   *(clockwise from top)* © Butch Martin Inc./The Image Bank; © Michael Melford/The Image Bank; © Gary Crallé/The Image Bank; © Benn Mitchell/The Image Bank; © Janeart Ltd./The Image Bank
59   © 1988 Environmental Defense Fund

Authors' acknowledgments

We would like to thank our **reviewers** for their helpful suggestions: Fred Anderson, Masashi Negishi, Chuck Sandy, and Penny Ur.

We would also like to acknowledge the students and teachers in the following schools and institutes who piloted components of *Active Listening: Building Skills for Understanding:*

Alianza Cultural Uruguay – Estados Unidos, Montevideo, Uruguay; **Central Washington University**, Washington, USA; **Drexel University**, Philadelphia, Pennsylvania, USA; **Fairmont State College**, Fairmont, West Virginia, USA; **Fu Jen University**, Taipei, Taiwan; **Gunma Prefectural Women's University,** Japan; **Impact Institute**, Santiago, Chile; **Kyoto YMCA (Central Branch)**, Kyoto, Japan; **Miyagi Gakuin Women's College**, Sendai, Japan; **Miyagi Gakuin High School**, Sendai, Japan; **National Yunlin Polytechnic Institute**, Yunlin, Taiwan; **Queen Alexandra Senior School**, Toronto, Canada; **Santa Clara Educational Options**, Santa Clara, California, USA; **Sendai YMCA English School**, Sendai, Japan; **Suzugamine Women's College**, Hiroshima City, Japan; **Technos International Academy**, Tokyo, Japan; **Tokyo Air Travel School**, Tokyo, Japan; **University of Iowa**, Iowa City, Iowa, USA; **University of Pittsburgh English Language Institute**, Pittsburgh, Pennsylvania, USA; **University of South Carolina**, Columbia, South Carolina, USA; **Wen Tzao Ursuline Junior College of Modern Languages**, Taiwan.

Thanks also go to Carmen Begay, Chuck Brochetti, Gerald Couzens, John Day, Marion Delarche, Harumi Fukuda, Brenda Hayashi, Ann Jenkins, Chris Johannes, Kaori Kato, Yuko Kato, Lalitha Manuel, Brian Matisz, Shelly McEvoy, Lionel Menasche, Hiroyuki Miyawaki, Mary Naby, Mark Porter, Sharon Setoguchi, Dorolyn Smith, Noriko Suzuki, Kazue Takahashi, Joseph Tomei, and Paul Wadden.

Finally, a special thanks to Suzette André, Mark Chesnut, David Fisher, Deborah Goldblatt, Sandra Graham, Steven Maginn, Susan Ryan, Ellen Shaw, and Mary Vaughn at Cambridge University Press.

Students' introduction

Welcome to *Active Listening: Building Skills for Understanding*. We hope this book will help you learn to listen to English more effectively. You'll practice listening to English. At the same time, you'll learn "how to listen." That is, you'll learn to make use of the English you already know. You'll also think about your reasons for listening. When you do that, listening and understanding become much easier.

This book has twenty units. Each unit has five parts:

- **Warming Up** Warming Up activities will help you remember what you know about the unit topic. This is an important step. It helps you get ready for listening.
- **Listening Task 1** You will listen to people in many different situations. Sometimes you'll listen for specific information such as numbers and places. Other times, you'll have to use what you hear to figure out things that aren't said directly. For example, you'll need to decide how strongly people feel about things they like and dislike.
- **Culture Corner** This is a short reading. It gives information about the unit topic.
- **Listening Task 2** Listening Task 2 is on the same theme as Listening Task 1, but it is a little more challenging.
- **Your Turn to Talk** This is a speaking activity. You will use the language you have just heard. You will do this task in pairs or small groups.

Hints to make you a better listener

- Think about the reason you are listening. Ask yourself, "What do I need to find out?" As you listen, you will do many different tasks. How you listen depends on what you need to find out. Each unit of the book will help you learn to listen. The first unit is called "Before You Begin." It introduces different types of listening. In Units 1–20, every listening task has a box in the top-right corner that tells you the purpose of the activity. The box will help you know what you are listening for.
- The tapes that go with this book are very natural. You won't be able to understand every word. Remember that you don't need to. People don't listen for every word, even in their native languages. The important thing is to think about the meaning of what you hear. You'll understand the most important words. That will help you follow the conversations.
- Many students worry about vocabulary. Of course, vocabulary is important. However, usually you don't need to look up new words in your dictionary the first time you meet them. Here's a good technique: When you hear a word for the first time, ignore it. The second time, try to guess the meaning. If by the third time you listen you still aren't sure, then look it up. This technique will make you more independent.

We hope you enjoy using this book and that you learn how to learn to be a more active, effective listener.

Teacher's introduction

Active Listening: Building Skills for Understanding is a course for low-intermediate to intermediate students of North American English. As the name implies, the course recognizes that listening is a very active process. Learners bring knowledge to class and perform a wide variety of interactive tasks. *Active Listening* can be used as the main text for listening classes or as a supplement in speaking or integrated skills classes.

ABOUT THE BOOK

The book includes twenty units, each with a warm-up activity; two main listening tasks; Culture Corner, a reading passage that presents information related to the unit theme; and Your Turn to Talk, a short speaking activity done in pairs or small groups. In addition, there is an introductory lesson called "Before You Begin." This lesson introduces learning strategies and types of listening, including listening for gist and inference. The lesson is particularly useful for learners whose previous experience has been limited primarily to listening for specific information or to answering literal comprehension questions.

The units can be taught in the order presented or out of sequence to follow the themes of the class or another book it is supplementing. In general, the tasks in the second half of the book are more challenging than those in the first.

Unit organization

Each unit begins with an activity called **Warming Up**. This activity, usually done in pairs, serves to remind learners of the language they already know. The tasks are designed to activate prior knowledge or "schemata." In the process of doing the warm-up activity, students work from their knowledge and, at the same time, use vocabulary and structures that are connected with a particular function or grammar point. The exercise makes the

listening tasks it precedes easier because the learners are prepared.

Listening Task 1 and **Listening Task 2** are the major listening exercises. The tasks are balanced to include a variety of listening types including listening for gist, identifying specific information, and understanding inferences. The purpose of each task is identified in a box in the top-right corner of each page. Because *Active Listening* features a task-based approach, learners should be doing the activities as they listen, rather than waiting until they have finished listening to a particular segment. To make this easier, writing is kept to a minimum. In most cases, students check boxes, number items, or write only words or short phrases.

Culture Corner is a short reading passage on the theme of the unit. In most cases, you'll want to use it as homework or as a break in classroom routine. Each Culture Corner ends with one or two discussion questions.

Your Turn to Talk, the final section of each unit, is a short, fluency-oriented speaking task done in pairs or small groups. In general, corrections are not appropriate during these activities. However, you may want to note common mistakes and, at the end of the period, write them on the board. Encourage learners to correct themselves.

Hints and techniques

■ Be sure to do the Warming Up section for each unit. This preview can foster a very healthy learning strategy. It teaches students "how to listen." Also, it makes students more successful, which, in turn, motivates and encourages them.

■ In general, you'll only want to play a particular segment one or two times. If the learners are still having difficulty, try telling them the answers. Then play the tape again and let them experience understanding what they heard.

■ If some students find listening very difficult, have them do the task in pairs, helping each other as necessary when possible. The Teacher's Edition contains additional ideas.

■ Some students may not be used to active learning. Those learners may be confused by instructions since they are used to taking a more passive role. Explaining activities is usually the least effective way to give instructions. It is better to demonstrate. For example, give the instruction as briefly as possible (e.g., "Listen. Number the pictures."). Then play the first part of the tape. Stop the tape and elicit the correct answer from the learners. Those who weren't sure what to do will quickly understand. The same technique works for Warming Up and Your Turn to Talk. Lead one pair or group through the first step of the task. The other learners watch. They quickly see what they are supposed to do.

Active Listening: Building Skills for Understanding is accompanied by a *Teacher's Edition* that contains a complete tapescript, step-by-step lesson plans, and expansion activities, as well as grammar and general notes.

FEATURES OF THE TEACHER'S EDITION

In addition to detailed teaching procedures for each activity, every unit of the Teacher's Edition also includes Notes, Additional Support activities, a Strategy Exercise, and Optional (listening/speaking) Activities.

The **Notes** include cultural information. They define idiomatic usage and provide grammatical explanations where appropriate.

The **Additional Support** activities provide another chance to listen and another purpose for listening. They may be used with classes that have a difficult time with listening.

The **Strategy Exercise** is designed to help students become more aware of their own language learning strategies and ways that they learn best. It will also make them aware that many different ways to learn exist. One

language learning strategy might be to associate vocabulary with physical actions. For example, if students are learning action verbs, you might have them pantomime the actions as they repeat the words to themselves. (This particular Strategy Exercise is suggested in Unit 3 of this Teacher's Edition.)

Strategies for learning a new language are not new. Good language learners have always used a variety of techniques to make progress. However, it is only recently that the field of English language teaching has begun to look at strategies in an organized way. Like any new aspect of teaching, strategies are promising, but they are not a magic key that will open every door.

We encourage you to look at the **Strategy Exercises** as you would any other language learning/awareness activity. Pick and choose. Select those you think would be of interest to your students. In general, encourage students to experiment with different ways to learn.

The **Optional Activities** are task-based listening/speaking activities that may be done any time during or after completion of a unit. They give students a chance to use the language they have been hearing.

HOW STUDENTS LEARN TO LISTEN

Many students find listening to be one of the most difficult skills in English. The following explains some of the ideas incorporated into the book to make students more effective listeners. *Active Listening: Building Skills for Understanding* is designed to help learners make real and rapid progress. Recent research into teaching listening and its related receptive skill, reading, have given insights into how successful students learn foreign/second languages.

Bottom-up vs. top-down processing, a brick-wall analogy*

To understand what our students are going through as they learn to listen or read, consider the "bottom-up vs. top-down processing" distinction. The distinction is based on the

*Thanks to Brian Tomlinson for suggesting the use of the brick-wall analogy to explain top-down/bottom-up processing.

ways learners process and attempt to understand what they read or hear. With bottom-up processing, students start with the component parts: words, grammar, and the like. Top-down processing is the opposite. Students start from their background knowledge.

This might be better understood by means of a metaphor. Imagine a brick wall. If you are standing at the bottom looking at the wall brick by brick, you can easily see the details. It is difficult, however, to get an overall view of the wall. And, if you come to a missing brick (e.g., an unknown word or unfamiliar structure), you're stuck. If, on the other hand, you're sitting on the top of the wall, you can easily see the landscape. Of course, because of distance, you'll miss some details.

Students, particularly those with years of "classroom English" but little experience in really using the language, try to listen from the bottom up.

They attempt to piece the meaning together, word by word. It is difficult for us, as native and advanced non-native English users, to experience what learners go through. However, try reading the following *from right to left.*

> word one ,slowly English process you When to easy is it ,now doing are you as ,time a at .word individual each of meaning the catch understand to difficult very is it ,However .passage the of meaning overall the

You were probably able to understand the paragraph:

> When you process English slowly, one word at a time, as you are doing now, it is easy to catch the meaning of each individual word. However, it is very difficult to understand the overall meaning of the passage.

While reading, however, it is likely that you felt the frustration of bottom-up processing; you had to get each individual part before you could make sense of it. This is similar to what

our students experience – and they're having to wrestle with the meaning in a foreign language. Of course, this is an ineffective way to listen since it takes too long. While students are still trying to make sense of what has been said, the speaker keeps going. The students get lost.

Although their processing strategy is a negative, students do come to class with certain strengths. From their years of English study, most have a relatively large, if passive, vocabulary. They also often have a solid receptive knowledge of English grammar. We shouldn't neglect the years of life experience; our learners bring with them a wealth of background knowledge on many topics. These three strengths – vocabulary, grammar, and life experience – can be the tools for effective listening.

The Warming Up activities in *Active Listening* build on those strengths. By engaging the students in active, meaningful prelistening tasks, students integrate bottom-up and top-down processing. They start from meaning, but, in the process of doing the task, they use vocabulary and structures (grammar) connected with the task, topic, or function. The result is an integrated listening strategy.

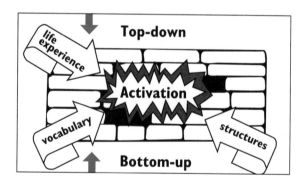

Types of Listening

A second factor that is essential in creating effective listeners is exposing them to a variety of types of listening. Many students have only had experience with listening for literal comprehension. While listening for specific information is an important skill, it represents only one type. We have attempted to reach a balance in the book in order to give students experience with – and an understanding of – listening for gist and inference. Students usually are quick to understand the idea of listening for gist. They can easily imagine having to catch the general meaning of something they hear. Inference, on the other hand, can be more difficult. Take the following example (from the introductory unit, "Before You Begin"). The students hear the following conversation:

Man: Let's go outside. We could go for a walk. Maybe we could play tennis.
Woman: *(with a slight laugh)* Look out the window. It's raining.
Man: Raining! Oh no!

At a gist level, students can easily identify "the weather" as the main topic of conversation. They are also able to pick out specific information, in this case, the fact that it's raining. To help students understand the idea of inference, ask them whether or not the people will go outside. Students understand that the weather is preventing them from going outside, even though neither the man nor the woman specifically says so.

Many of these ideas are helpful in understanding the listening process, but should not be seen as rigid models. We need to remember that listening is actually very complex. A student listening for gist or inference, for example, may get the clues from catching a couple of specific bits of information.

Of course, learners need practice in listening. But they need more: They need to learn *how* to listen. They need different types of listening strategies and tasks. They need to learn to preview. Our students need exposure to it all. When learners get the exposure they need, they build their listening skills. They become active listeners.

Marc Helgesen
Steven Brown

How do you learn English?

Dear students:

We hope that you learn a lot of English. We also hope that you enjoy learning it.

Do you ever think about how you learn? What things do you do to learn English? What techniques help you learn? There are many different ways to try to learn. These are called **strategies**. This book will teach you many different strategies. Think about how you learn best. Try to find the strategies that work best for you.

One strategy is **clarification**. When you ask for clarification, you are "trying to understand." For example, if you don't understand something, you can say, "Could you repeat that?"

Another strategy is **prediction**. Prediction is when you think about what will happen. You guess what you will hear.

In Listening Task 1, you will learn to ask for clarification. But first, try a prediction activity.

Work with a partner.
Look at Listening Task 1 on page 3.
You already know a lot of English.
What do you think the sentences will be?
Say the sentences.

Good luck with learning English. You can do it!

Sincerely,

Marc Helgesen
Steven Brown

How do you learn English?

> **Topic/function:** Explaining types of listening
> **Listening skills:** Clarification (Listening Task 1); listening types: gist, specific information, inferences (Listening Task 2)

Note: Throughout this Teacher's Edition, the symbol "T:" followed by *italic* type indicates the teacher's script.

From the people who wrote this book

I. Hold your book so that students can see page 2. T: *Look at page 2. This is a letter from the people who wrote this book. The letter will help you understand how to use the book.*

2. Read the letter aloud as the students read along silently. Stop before the last sentences to give students time to predict the sentences on the next page.

3. (**Optional**) To save time on Listening Task 1, you may want to have students write their answers as they do this preview task.

> **Note:** Do not have students say their predictions as a whole group yet. That is better saved until after they have done Listening Task 1.

NOTES

• The ideas in this unit may be new to many students. As you read the letter, pause after each sentence so that students have time to think about the meaning.

• The following words may be new to some students. That's why they are defined in the letter.

> **strategies:** ways to try to learn
> (**asking for**) **clarification:** trying to understand

> **prediction:** guessing what you think will happen

Students shouldn't worry if they don't completely understand the words after reading the letter. They will by the end of the lesson.

These words, along with the listening types presented in Listening Task 2, are fairly technical. While we have limited the number of such words taught in the book, having students know a few key terms can help them focus their learning. Having the students know these words also makes it easier for you as the teacher to direct students' attention to the purpose of each task.

Strategy exercise

Each unit of this *Teacher's Edition* introduces a language learning strategy designed to build students' awareness and control over their own learning. However, since the Before You Begin unit is entirely about listening strategies, an additional strategy is not recommended at this time.

The strategies in this unit are (a) prediction, (b) clarification, and (c) awareness of listening purpose (listening for gist, listening for specific information, understanding inferences).

Optional activities

(For use anytime during or after the unit.)

• *Memory game.* Students work in pairs. With their books closed, have students try to remember and write down as many of the clarification phrases on page 3 as they can.

• *Lipreading.* Ask students to look at the expressions on page 3. Put students in pairs. Tell them to say a phrase from the list *silently* (that is, they move their lips but say nothing aloud). Their partner will read their lips and guess the phrase. They then change partners and continue playing. Each student who guesses correctly gets one point.

Listening Task 1
What do you say when . . . ?

Listening skill: Clarification

Note: The tapescript for Before You Begin starts on page T1.

1. T: *Look at page 3. What do you say when . . . ?*

2. Read the instructions: *In English, when you don't understand something, you should ask. There are many ways to ask for clarification. Look at the questions. What do you think the sentences will be? Write them.*

3. As students work, circulate and help those having difficulty. If there are items they just can't guess, they should skip them and go on to the next item. You may want learners to do this step in pairs.

4. T: *Now listen. Were you right? Correct the sentences.* Play Listening Task 1 on the tape. Gesture for students to check their answers.

5. (**Optional**) You may wish to stop after each item and have the students say the sentences as you write them on the board.

6. If necessary, play Listening Task 1 a second time.

7. If not done in step 5 of this plan, check by having students say the answers as you write them on the board. (Answers appear in blue on the opposite page.)

NOTES

• Most students have previously learned these simple patterns. Many, however, aren't used to using them. The book begins with this activity to remind students that it is their responsibility to ask for clarification.

• Students predict their answers both to get practice with a very useful strategy and also to help them identify their own mistakes.

• In the cartoon, the teacher is speaking too rapidly without pausing, and this creates the confusion. He is actually saying, "In Listening Task 1 you will learn to ask for clarification."

Culture corner

Culture Corner is a short reading passage which appears at the bottom of each Listening Task 1 page. An optional activity for using the Culture Corner passage is given in every unit of this *Teacher's Edition*.

1. After students have read the passage, you may want to have them discuss the questions at the end of the passage: *In your country, is it OK to ask the teacher questions? How do you feel about asking questions in English?* You might choose to allow them to use their native language for this discussion.

2. (**Optional**) Many students know other ways to clarify. A useful follow-up is to have students work in groups of three to five. Have groups list as many ways to ask for clarification as they can. It will probably be helpful to set a time limit of about 5 minutes. Then, have each group call out their phrases as you write them on the board. If there are mistakes, simply write the phrase correctly without drawing attention to it. Finally, have students copy the list onto the inside cover of their books for easy reference. In future classes, when students need to clarify something and forget to use the English phrase, you can just gesture for them to look at the list they have written.

What do you say when . . . ?

In English, when you don't understand something, you should ask.
There are many ways to ask for clarification.

❑ Look at the questions. What do you think the sentences will be?
Write them.

❑ Now listen. Were you right? Correct the sentences.

What do you say when . . .

1. you want someone to say something again?
C_ould you_ r_epeat_ that?
E_xcuse_ m _e_?
P_ardon_ ?

2. you want to know how to spell a word?
How d _o_ _you_ spell (that)?

3. you want to know a word in English?
How _do_ _you_ say (that) in English?

4. you don't understand something?
I don't u _nderstand_ .

5. you understand the meaning but don't know
the answer?
_I_ _don't_ know.

6. you want the teacher to play the tape again?
Once m _ore_ p _lease_ .

In listening task 1 you will learn to ask for clarification.

Every culture has different "rules" about asking questions. In some countries, it is
bad to stop the teacher. It means that the teacher didn't explain something very
well. In English-speaking countries (and in English class), it is good – and
important – to stop the teacher or another student. It means you are interested
and are paying attention. In English, it is your job to ask if you don't understand.
In your country, is it OK to ask the teacher questions? How do you feel about
asking questions in English?

3

What are you listening for?

LISTENING TASK 2

There are many ways to listen. We listen differently for different reasons.

1 Sometimes, you have to understand only the topic or situation.

Example 1 ■ The topic
Listen to the conversation.
What is the most important idea?
Check (✔) your answer.

| friends | ✔ the weather | the window |

Example 2 ■ Shopping
Listen. Some people are in a clothing store.
What kind of clothes are they talking about?
Check (✔) your answer.

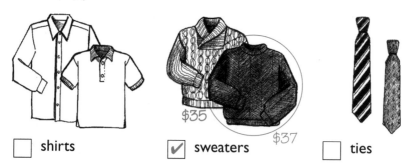

$35 $37

| shirts | ✔ sweaters | ties |

This is called **listening for gist**.
You don't need to understand everything. You just want the
general meaning.

Listening Task 2
What are you listening for?

> **Listening skills:** Listening for gist, listening for specific information, understanding inferences

1. T: *Look at pages 4 and 5.*

2. (**Optional**) Read the title: *"What are you listening for?" What do you think this activity will be about?* Elicit answers from the students. (Answer: listening types/purposes)

3. (**Optional**) If students find listening very difficult, do the Additional Support procedure.

4. Read the instructions: *There are many ways to listen. We listen differently for different reasons. Part 1. Sometimes, you have to understand only the topic or situation. Example 1: The topic. Listen to the conversation. What is the most important idea? Check your answer.*

5. Listen to Example 1 on the tape. Gesture for students to check the answer (the weather). Stop the tape after the example. Elicit the answer from the students. Note that the people on the tape are friends and that they mention the window, but the main idea is the weather.

6. Read the instructions and play the tape for Example 2. Elicit the answer (sweaters).

7. (**Optional**) Stop the tape and write "listening for gist" on the board. Make sure students understand the idea.

8. Continue in the same way with parts 2 and 3 of this activity on page 5. Read the instructions and play the tape segment for each part, then stop and review the answers.

9. After the inference items (part 3), it may be useful to talk about which words gave the students the answers. Example 1: raining; Example 2: easy to keep clean, show dirt, etc.

ADDITIONAL SUPPORT   Have students work in pairs. Before each illustrated example, have them look at the three pictures. They should say or write at least two words associated with the pictures.

NOTES

• Students may be surprised to hear the same tape segment used in Example 1 for all three parts. However, for most students it clearly illustrates how the reason for listening (the task) is different, even with the same bit of language.

• Of the three listening types mentioned here, "understanding inferences" is often the most difficult for learners. This is both because most students have had little experience with it; also it is the most abstract of the three. Assure the students that they will be given plenty of practice with all the types as they use this book.

• "Listening for gist" is also called "global listening" and "listening for the main idea."

• "Listening for specific information" is also called "listening for details" and "focused listening." It is useful for students to realize that listening for specific information does not mean understanding every word and picking out the information they need. Rather, it involves understanding the task and focusing in to catch that particular information.

See page 4 for the procedure for the listening activities on this page.

Your turn to talk

1. Divide the class into pairs. T: *Work in pairs. Try speaking only English for two minutes. Choose one of these topics:*

- *how I learn English,*
- *my free-time activities, or*
- *my family.*

Partner, make sure you understand. Look at page 3 and use as many clarification sentences as you can. Check the sentences each time you use them. Then change parts.

2. T: *Who will speak first? First speakers in each pair, raise your hand.* Gesture for them to begin.

3. (after 2 minutes) T: *Stop. Now the other speaker starts.*

4. (**Optional**) (after 2 minutes) T: *Stop. Now count how many times you used the phrases.*

2 Often, you have to understand specific information.

Example 1 ■ The weather
Listen. What is the weather like? Check (✔) your answer.

☐ It's sunny.　　　☐ It's snowing.　　　✔ It's raining.

Example 2 ■ Shopping
Look at the pictures of clothing on page 4.
Listen. How much do the sweaters cost? Write the prices below the pictures.

This is called **listening for specific information**.
Think about what information you need. Ask yourself, "What am I listening for?"

3 Sometimes, the speaker doesn't say the exact words, but you can still understand the meaning.

Example 1 ■ The weather
Listen. Will they go outside? Check (✔) your answer.

☐ Yes　　　　✔ No

Example 2 ■ Shopping
Look at the pictures of clothing on page 4.
Listen. Which sweater does the woman buy? Circle the one she buys.

This is called **understanding inferences**.
You can understand the meaning even though no one says the exact words.

YOUR TURN TO TALK

Work in pairs. Try speaking only English for two minutes. Choose one of these topics: how I learn English, my free-time activities, or my family. Partner, make sure you understand. Look at page 3 and use as many clarification sentences as you can. Check (✔) the sentences each time you use them. Then change parts.

Example
A: I learn English by watching TV.
B: Could you repeat that?
A: I learn English by watching TV. I always watch American movies . . .

Getting to know you

❑ Work with a partner.
Imagine these people are joining your class.

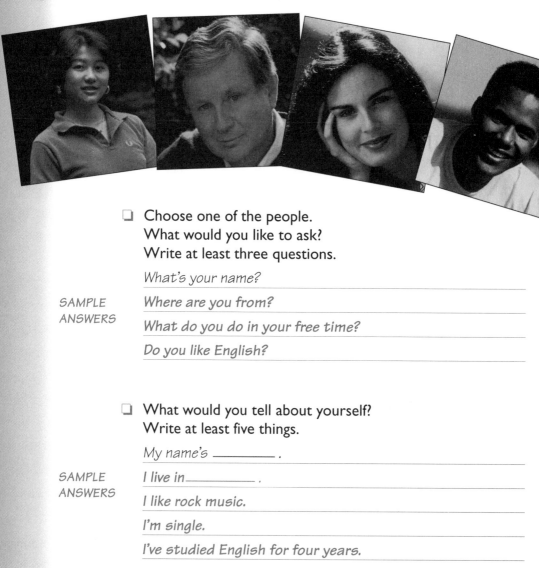

❑ Choose one of the people.
What would you like to ask?
Write at least three questions.

What's your name?

SAMPLE
ANSWERS

Where are you from?

What do you do in your free time?

Do you like English?

❑ What would you tell about yourself?
Write at least five things.

My name's _____ .

SAMPLE
ANSWERS

I live in _____ .

I like rock music.

I'm single.

I've studied English for four years.

❑ Change partners. Find a classmate you don't know very well.
Ask at least three questions.
Tell your new partner about yourself.

Getting to know you

> **Topic/funtion:** Meeting people
> **Listening skills:** Understanding questions, following instructions (Listening Task 1); identifying/inferring relationships (Listening Task 2)
> **Grammar/vocabulary:** *Wh-* questions (present), imperatives

Warming Up

1. Hold your book so that students can see page 6. T: *Look at page 6.*

2. Read the following instructions. Pause when you see the symbol ♦ to give students time to answer the questions.

> *Work with a partner.*
> *Imagine these people are joining your class.*
> *Choose one of the people.*
> *What would you like to ask?*
> *Write at least three questions.* ♦

3. Demonstrate by asking several students: *Who did you choose? What would you ask him (or her)?*

4. Continue with the script:

> *What would you tell about yourself?*
> *Write at least five things.* ♦
> *Change partners. Find a classmate you don't know very well.*
> *Ask at least three questions.*
> *Tell your new partner about yourself.*

5. As students work, circulate and help pairs having difficulty. Check the understanding of those pairs by asking questions like these:

> *Which person would you like to meet?*
> *What would you say about yourself?*

If students are unsure what to ask during the last part of the activity, point to the questions they wrote and indicate that they should ask them.

6. Check responses by having students call out the questions and things about themselves. You may want to write the questions on the chalkboard. For the information about themselves, write the basic patterns. Write blanks for the information that varies (e.g., I like _____).

NOTES

• The purpose of Warming Up is to "activate" (remind the students of) words, grammar, and content they already know. In most cases, mistakes in grammar should be ignored at this time unless they make understanding difficult. It is better to simply repeat the sentence correctly. The students will be hearing correct models many times during the unit.

• Most students will be familiar with *Wh-* questions. Remind them that the kind of questions people ask depends on culture, the setting, and their relationship with the other person. For example, in English-speaking cultures, one usually doesn't ask about age or salary when meeting someone for the first time.

• *Imperatives.* In Listening Task 1, the instructions ask the students to write certain things on the page. They use the command form: "Write . . . " The imperative is usually used to give orders (Stop!), to make suggestions (Take some aspirin.), and to encourage people to do something (Have a drink.).

• "Please" is not always used in commands in school settings; a friendly tone of voice is usually polite enough.

Optional activity

(For use anytime during or after the unit.)

• *Your name is . . .* Divide the class into groups of ten to twelve students. Tell them to arrange themselves in alphabetical order according to their first names. The first group to finish correctly wins. Play again with last names.

Listening Task 1   How about you?

Note: The tapescript for Unit 1 begins on page T3.

1. T: *Look at page 7.*

2. (Optional) Read the title: *"How about you?" What do you think this activity will be about?* Elicit answers from the students. (Answer: information about themselves)

3. (Optional) If students find listening very difficult, do the Additional Support procedure.

4. Read the instructions: *Listen. Write answers about yourself.*

5. Play Listening Task 1 on the tape. Gesture for students to write their answers.

   Note: Some students are not used to activities where they supply real information about themselves. Make sure they understand that the tape contains only the questions. They provide the answers.

6. (Optional) To make sure students understand what to do, stop after one or two questions. Ask two or three students: *What did you write in the circle? What did you write in the triangle?* Then play the rest of Listening Task 1.

7. If necessary, play Listening Task 1 a second time.

8. Check by asking several students their answers for each item. You may want to write the topics on the board in the correct positions. (Topics appear in blue on the opposite page.)

9. As you check, encourage learners to give extra information about their answers (e.g., if a student has written "China" for item 1, ask: *Do you think you'll go there someday? What do you want to see?*).

ADDITIONAL SUPPORT Write the *Wh-*question words (who, what, when, where, why) on the board. Have students listen once with their books closed. As they listen, they should try to see how often they hear those words. Also, they should note any topics they think are mentioned (friends, countries, etc.).

Culture corner

1. After students have read the Culture Corner, have them work in pairs to answer the question: *What would you call the people in the pictures below?* (Answers: Ms. Weldon, Bill, Dr. Sato)

2. (Optional) Have students work in small groups and compare the use of titles in their own country. One way is to have them list as many titles as possible and identify who they would call by each. In most languages, the relationship of the speakers as well as the situation determines when titles are used.

Strategy exercise: *Recognizing and using common patterns*

Every language is full of set phrases and common patterns. One way to become a better listener is to learn to anticipate and recognize these patterns. If a listening activity is about introductions and meeting people, we expect to hear, "John, this is Mary. Mary, John. Mary works in my department." Learning to anticipate these set phrases can decrease work necessary when listening. Knowing where the phrases are likely to be used allows students to get ready for the information they need.

   To get this point across, before listening to Listening Task 2, have students look at page 8 for 30 seconds. Then they close their books. On the board write a list of places students think the conversations might be taking place. Then, in small groups, students list things strangers might talk about and things friends might talk about. Ask students how these people might begin a conversation.

LISTENING TASK 1

How about you?

❑ Listen. Write answers about yourself.

1.
(country)

2.
(friend's name)

3.
(hometown)

4.
(free-time activity)

5.
(something they dislike)

6.
(favorite subject)

7.
(favorite music)

8.
(something they like)

CULTURE CORNER

Titles like *Mr.*, *Ms.*, and *Dr.* are usually not used when you say only the person's first name. You might call Tom Johnson *Mr. Johnson* but not *Mr. Tom.* The title *Ms.* is used for both single and married women. Use *Ms.* unless a woman tells you she prefers *Miss* or *Mrs.* What would you call the people in the pictures below?

Amy
Weldon
(your
teacher)

Bill
Jones
(your best
friend)

Jane
Sato
(your
doctor)

7

Friends or strangers?

❏ Listen. Are these people friends or strangers?
Write "F" for "friends" and "S" for "strangers."

1. ___F___

2. ___S___

3. ___F___

4. ___S___

5. ___S___

6. ___S___

 **YOUR TURN TO TALK**

Work with a partner. Look at your partner's answers to Listening Task 1, "How about you?" on page 7. Which answers are interesting? Ask questions about the answers. Try to learn at least five new things about your partner.

Sample questions

What does this mean?

Why do you want to go there?

Where did you meet _____*(name)*_____ ?

How often do you . . . ?

Listening Task 2
Friends or strangers?

Listening skills: Identifying/inferring relationships

I. T: *Look at page 8.*

2. (**Optional**) Read the title: *"Friends or strangers?" What do you think this activity will be about?* Elicit answers from the students. (Answer: deciding whether or not people know each other)

3. (**Optional**) If students find listening very difficult, do the Additional Support procedure.

4. Read the instructions: *Listen. Are these people friends or strangers? Write "F" for "friends" and "S" for "strangers."*

5. Play Listening Task 2 on the tape. Gesture for students to write "F" or "S" on the lines.

6. (**Optional**) To make sure students understand what to do, stop after the first item. *They're friends. How did you know?* (Answer: They're in an office, talking about what they did over the weekend.) Then play the rest of Listening Task 2.

7. If necessary, play Listening Task 2 a second time. Before replaying the tape, you may want to have students compare their answers in pairs. *Work with a partner. Look at your partner's answers. How many were the same? Then we'll listen again.*

8. Check by eliciting answers from the students or by having them raise their hands. (Answers appear in blue on the opposite page.)

ADDITIONAL SUPPORT Have students listen once with their books closed. As they listen, they should note how many speakers are men and how many are women. They can also try to catch hints about the location or topic of each conversation. Of course, noting the number of men and women isn't directly related to the task of identifying relationships. It does, however, give students a clear, achievable goal as well as provide a chance to listen an extra time.

NOTE

• You may prefer to check after each segment rather than waiting until students have heard all six parts. If you ask the follow-up questions suggested in step 8, the students will be able to hear the listening strategies and clues their classmates are using.

Your turn to talk

I. Divide the class into pairs. T: *Work with a partner. You will learn more about your partner.*

2. T: *Look at page 7 in your partner's book. Read about your partner. Ask your partner more questions.*

3. (after about 5 minutes) T: *Pairs, join another pair. Work in groups of four. Introduce your partner to the new people.*

Optional activity

(For use anytime during or after the unit.)

• *Quick questions.* Review the kinds of questions practiced in this unit. Ask students to remember the questions they asked during Warming Up. Write some of the questions on the board. Put the students in groups of ten to twelve. Give each group a ball or paper that has been crumpled into a ball. The first student should throw the ball to anyone he or she wishes. Before throwing the ball, that student asks a question (e.g., Who is your favorite singer?"). The person catching the ball must answer as quickly as possible. That student is the next to throw the ball.

What's your number?

> **Topic/function:** Asking for and giving (numerical) information
> **Listening skills:** Understanding and processing numbers (Listening Tasks 1 and 2)
> **Grammar/vocabulary:** Numbers

Warming Up

1. Hold your book so that students can see page 9. T: *Look at page 9.*

2. Read the following instructions. Pause when you see the symbol ♦ to give students time to answer the questions.

> *Write these numbers.*
> *Your telephone number.* ♦
> *Your address.* ♦
> *What other numbers are important to you?*
> *Dates? Times? Ages? Prices? Height?*
> *What else? Write some of them. Don't write*
> *what they mean. Don't write any "secret"*
> *numbers like bank accounts.* ♦

3. As students work, circulate and work with those having difficulty. If some students can't think of numbers that apply to them, have the whole class brainstorm types of numbers. Write them on the board. T: *What kinds of numbers could you write?* (Possible answers: birthdays, student identification numbers, video or sports club membership numbers)

4. After a few minutes, continue with the second part of the activity: *Work with a partner. Read your numbers. Partner, write the numbers you hear. Then say what you think they mean.*

NOTES

• The purpose of this activity is to get students thinking about numbers and how to say them in English. Stress to the students that they should not say any secret numbers.

• An alternative way to teach the second part of the activity is to have all students choose one of their numbers that is interesting or challenging. Students stand and circulate. They form pairs. Each reads the chosen number. The partner writes it and guesses the meaning. They then change partners and continue. You may want to allow them to give hints, either with words or gestures. To do the activity as a game, the winner is either the first person to collect and guess the meaning of numbers from ten other people or the person who collects the most numbers in a set amount of time.

• Some students might initially be surprised to see a unit on numbers in a book at this level. Numbers are usually taught at a beginning stage. To really master numbers, students need a lot of practice. Most intermediate students still have difficulty, especially with larger numbers.

• There are many ways to say numbers in English: "104" might be "one hundred four," "a hundred and four," or "one-oh-four," depending on the individual speaker. Sometimes when a number is repeated, the speaker will say it differently the second time to help the listener better understand: "One hundred four." "That's one-oh-four."

• Telephone numbers, social security numbers, and other numbers with hyphens usually have a characteristic pattern when spoken. First, the speaker says each number separately: 555 is read as "five-five-five." The speaker pauses: Five-five-five (pause) seven-two-oh-five.

• In telephone numbers, "0" is usually pronounced "oh" rather than "zero."

• In North American English, the usual order for dates is month/day/year.

What's your number?

WARMING UP

❑ Write these numbers.

SAMPLE ANSWERS

Your telephone number: _555-4637_

Your address: _5-15-21 Yoshinari_

Chuo-ku, Osaka 541

❑ What other numbers are important to you?
   Dates? Times? Ages? Prices? Height? What else?
   Write some of them. Don't write what they mean.
   Don't write any "secret" numbers like bank accounts.

SAMPLE
ANSWERS

June 3	555-7205
8:15	220-98-2133
21	5225

❑ Work with a partner.
   Read your numbers.
   Partner, write the numbers you hear.
   Then say what you think they mean.

May I ask your number?

❏ Listen. Find the correct form for each conversation.
Write the missing numbers in the correct places.

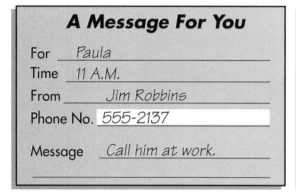

FIRST CLASS

To   *Eri Sato*
Street   *3209 West 145th Street*

City   *Los Angeles, CA*
ZIP Code   *90025*

a. a mailing label

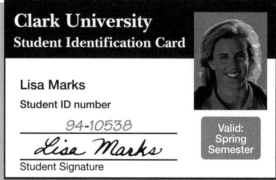

VISTA CARD

4122   *34862 212039 62008*

VALID FROM
FIRST DAY OF
05/95

GOOD THRU
LAST DAY OF
03/97 CV

TOM DAVIS

VISTA

b. a credit card

A Message For You

For   *Paula*
Time   *11 A.M.*
From   *Jim Robbins*
Phone No. *555-2137*

Message   *Call him at work.*

c. a telephone message pad

Clark University
Student Identification Card

Lisa Marks

Student ID number

94-10538

Lisa Marks

Student Signature

Valid:
Spring
Semester

d. a student ID card

CULTURE CORNER

Different cultures have different lucky and unlucky numbers. In Western countries, thirteen is an unlucky number. Some hotels do not have a thirteenth floor. In Japan, four is an unlucky number because it sounds like the word for "death." Double sixes (66) is very lucky in China because it sounds like "everything goes well." In Thailand, three and nine (3 2 3) are good numbers. People in India say odd numbers (3, 5, 7, . . .) are lucky. What numbers are lucky in your country? Unlucky? Do you have a lucky number?

Listening Task 1
May I ask your number?

Note: The tapescript for Unit 2 begins on page T4.

1. T: *Look at page 10.*

2. (**Optional**) Read the title: *"May I ask your number?" What do you think this will be about?* Elicit answers from the students. (Answer: personal numbers)

3. (**Optional**) If students find listening very difficult, do the Additional Support procedure below.

4. Read the instructions: *Listen. Find the correct form for each conversation. Write the missing numbers in the correct places.*

5. Play Listening Task 1 on the tape. Gesture for students to write their answers.

6. (**Optional**) To make sure students understand what to do, stop after the first two items. Ask students: *What is Lisa's identification number?* (94-10538). Then play the rest of Listening Task 1.

7. If necessary, play Listening Task 1 a second time.

8. Check by having students call out the numbers as you write them on the board. (Answers appear in blue on the opposite page.)

ADDITIONAL SUPPORT Have students close their books. On a piece of paper, have them write the numbers 0 to 9. As they listen, they cross out each number they hear.

NOTES

• ZIP codes are postal codes. Each area in the United States has a nine-digit ZIP code, though most people use only the first five numbers.

Culture corner

1. After students have read the Culture Corner, you may wish to have them, in small groups, compare their answers to the questions. *What numbers are lucky in your country? Unlucky? Do you have a lucky number?*

2. (**Optional**) Students can also decide how they would explain why certain numbers are lucky or unlucky in their cultures. How are the numbers used or avoided (e.g., hotel floors and room numbers, not giving gifts containing a certain number of items, etc.)?

Strategy exercise: *Listening with a purpose*

Each time they listen, students need to know why they are listening. You can use hypothetical situations to help students learn this skill. Students can work in pairs to answer this question: "In your own language, what do you listen to each day?" Some answers might be: "I listen to the weather report on the radio in the morning." "I listen to my teacher tell me about the homework." "I listen to my friend tell me about what she did last night." After students list the ways they listen, have them write down the information they listen for (e.g., in the weather report, the temperature or whether it's going to rain).

Optional activity

(For use anytime during or after the unit.)

• *Buzz.* Go around the class, counting to 100. Each student says one number. The rule: Don't say a number with a 3 in it (13, 23, 31, etc.). Also don't say any number that you can divide by 3 (3, 6, 9, etc.). Instead, say "buzz." Example: One. Two. Buzz. Four. Five. Buzz. Seven . . . Try it again. This time, leave out 7s.

Listening Task 2 Fast math

Listening skill: Understanding and processing numbers

1. T: *Look at page 11.*

2. (**Optional**) Read the title: *"Fast math."* *What do you think this will be about?* Elicit answers from the students. (Answer: a math race)

3. Read the instructions: *Listen. Write the numbers. How fast can you figure out the answers? Try to write the answers before you hear them.*

4. Play Listening Task 2 on the tape. Gesture for students to write and add or multiply the numbers. (**Optional**) If students find listening very difficult, do the Additional Support procedure below.

5. (**Optional**) To make sure students understand what to do, stop after the musical scale on item 2 (before the answer is given). Ask: *What's the answer?* (Answer: 5,337) Then play the rest of Listening Task 2.

6. If necessary, play Listening Task 2 a second time. Before replaying the tape, you may want to have students compare their answers in pairs. *Work with a partner. Look at your partner's answers. How many were the same? Then we'll listen again.*

7. Check by having students call out the answers. Write them on the board. (Answers appear in blue on the opposite page.)

ADDITIONAL SUPPORT Preteach the words "plus" and "times" if you think students don't know them. Have them do step 4 in pairs. Stop the tape each time you hear the music. Let them compare answers before they hear the correct answer on the tape.

NOTES

• You may prefer to check after each segment rather than waiting until students have heard all eight parts.

• Ways to say arithmetic functions: $5 + 8$, five plus eight; $8 - 5$, eight minus five (children often say "eight take away five") ; 8×5, eight times five; $8 \div 5$, eight divided by five.

Your turn to talk

1. Divide the class into groups of four. T: *Work in groups of four. Each person in the group says a number larger than 100. Write the numbers. Then add them. Who can add the fastest?.*

2. Demonstrate with one group as the others watch. Direct each student to say a number. Encourage them to add quickly.

3. After about 5 minutes, stop the activity.

Optional activity

(For use anytime during or after the unit.)

• *1–100.* Students work in pairs. Enlarge and copy the number grid below (or have each pair write the numbers 1–100 on a piece of paper). Each pair needs one copy. Students cross out all numbers somehow related to themselves (dates, ID numbers, addresses, etc.). The pair that crosses out the most numbers is the winner.

1	2	3	4	5	6	7	8	9	10
11	12	13	14	15	16	17	18	19	20
21	22	23	24	25	26	27	28	29	30
31	32	33	34	35	36	37	38	39	40
41	42	43	44	45	46	47	48	49	50
51	52	53	54	55	56	57	58	59	60
61	62	63	64	65	66	67	68	69	70
71	72	73	74	75	76	77	78	79	80
81	82	83	84	85	86	87	88	89	90
91	92	93	94	95	96	97	98	99	100

LISTENING TASK 2 *Fast math*

❏ Listen. Write the numbers.
How fast can you figure out the answers?
Try to write the answers before you hear them.

1.	389	**2.**	1,877	**3.**	4,852

1.   389
\+   56
——————
    445

2.   1,877
\+ 3,460
——————
  5,337

3.   4,852
\+ 2,911
——————
  7,763

4.   128
×   3
——————
   384

5.   746
×   5
——————
  3,730

6.   1,857
×   7
——————
 12,999

❏ Now listen to two conversations in a department store.
Figure out the totals before you hear them.
Write the prices.

7. $ 19.95
×   3
——————
$ 59.85

8. $ 35.50
\+ 23.77
——————
$ 59.27

YOUR TURN TO TALK

Work in groups of four. Each person in the group says a number larger than 100.
Write the numbers. Then add them. Who can add the fastest? Did you all get the
same total? Continue with new numbers.

Example
A: 125
B: 242
C: 560
D: 329
B: I got 1257.
C: No, that's not right. It's 1256.

I'm hungry!

WARMING **UP**

What is your favorite food?
How do you make it?

❏ Work with a partner.
Tell your partner how to make the food.
Use some of these words:

bake

boil

peel

cut

slice

chop

fry

stir

put in

Food: *Apple pie*   SAMPLE ANSWER

First, *peel the apples and slice them.*

Then, *put them in a bowl.*

Next, *add cinnamon and sugar and stir.*

After that, *put the apples in the pie crust.*

Finally, *bake the pie for about an hour.*

U N I T 3
I'm hungry!

Topic/function: Explaining how to make a
food
Listening skills: Following instructions
(Listening Task 1); identifying a
sequence (Listening Task 2)
Grammar/vocabulary: Imperatives,
sequence markers

Warming Up

1. Hold your book so the students can see
page 12. T: *Look at page 12.*

2. Read the following instructions. Pause
when you see the symbol ♦ to give
students time to answer the questions.

> *What is your favorite food? How do you make
> it?*
> *Work with a partner.*
> *Tell your partner how to make the food.*
> *Use some of these words: bake, boil, peel, cut,
> slice, chop, fry, stir, put in.* ♦

3. Demonstrate by asking two or three
students: *What's your favorite food? How do
you make it?* Have students say the first one
or two steps in making the food.

4. Have students work in pairs. T: *Work
with a partner. Tell you partner how to make the
food.*

5. As students work, circulate and help
pairs having difficulty. Check the
understanding of those pairs by asking
questions like these: *What food do you know
how to make? What do you do first? What's
next?*

NOTES

• Some students may say they don't know
how to cook. However, nearly everyone
can make something simple like a
sandwich or a cup of coffee or tea.

• This unit is concerned with process
language. It uses cooking as an example.

Although your students may not be expert
cooks, everyone has made a sandwich at
one time. Encourage your students to
break down their experiences into short
steps and to be specific.

Strategy exercise: *Action and vocabulary*

One way to remember new vocabulary is to
associate it with physical actions. Some of
the cooking verbs on page 12 may be new.
Have students select those words that are
new and pantomime the actions as they
repeat the words to themselves.

Optional activities

(For use anytime during or after the unit.)

• *Menu role play.* Have students work in
pairs to write down a menu. The menu
should include some of their favorite
foods. One student is the waiter. The other
is the customer. The waiter decides which
foods the restaurant has. The customer
orders. If the restaurant is out of a dish,
the customer should order another. You
may want to put a model dialogue on the
chalkboard.

• *World food.* Students should look at the
world map on pages 66 and 67. In pairs,
they list as many foods from other
countries as they can in a short time (5 to
7 minutes). The team with the most foods
listed is the winner.

Listening Task 1
Now that's a sandwich!

Listening skill: Following instructions

Note: The tapescript for Unit 3 begins on page T5.

1. T: *Look at page 13.*

2. (**Optional**) Read the title: *"Now that's a sandwich! "What do you think this will be about?* Elicit answers from the students. (Answer: making a very large sandwich)

3. (**Optional**) If students find listening very difficult, do the Additional Support procedure below.

4. Read the instructions: *Listen. What ingredients go in this sandwich? Write or draw them.*

5. Play Listening Task 1 on the tape. Gesture for students to write their answers.

6. (**Optional**) To make sure students understand what to do, stop after one or two ingredients are mentioned. Ask two or three students: *What was first? What's next?* (Answers: roast beef, turkey) Write them on the board. Then play the rest of Listenng Task 1.

7. If necessary, play Listening Task 1 a second time.

8. Check students' answers by drawing the bottom piece of bread on the board. Have students call out the ingredients in order (from bottom to top). Write the words on the board. (Answers appear in blue on the opposite page.)

ADDITIONAL SUPPORT As a full class, brainstorm possible ingredients for a sandwich. List as many as possible on the board. Have students close their books. Play the tape. Have them listen and see how many of the listed ingredients they hear.

Alternatively, students can brainstorm in pairs or groups of three. They see how many ingredients they can list in about 3 minutes. One way to do this is to have them draw a line down the center of the page. They write ingredients on the right side. Then, as they listen to the tape, they simply draw arrows to show the position of any items they previously listed. They write or draw the additional items.

NOTES

• Some students may take too much time if they choose to draw the ingredients. This is especially true of those who are good artists and want the pictures perfect. It may be useful to forbid the use of erasers. Once a line is drawn, it can't be changed. This will help them work faster.

• If you feel your students do not know the ingredients for the sandwich, bring in pictures. Better yet, bring in the real things to encourage interest. Then, as a review, have a student make the sandwich in front of the class as other students remind her or him of the instructions they heard.

Ingredients/pictures you will need: bread, roast beef, turkey, onions, tomatoes, mushrooms, cheese, lettuce, mustard.

Culture corner

1. After they have read the Culture Corner, you may want to ask students the questions: *Are sandwiches popular in your country? What kind?*

2. (**Optional**) Have students work in pairs. They each change three or four words in the paragraph (e.g., ". . . two pieces of bread with something in the middle – cheese, fish, or vegetables."). They read their changed paragraphs to each other. Partners try to find the changes. If the listeners have their books open, it is an intensive reading/listening activity. If books are closed, it becomes a memory game.

Now that's a sandwich!

❑ Listen. What ingredients go in this sandwich?
Write or draw them.

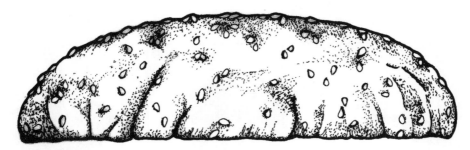

Mustard

Lettuce

Cheese

Mushrooms

Tomatoes

Onions

Turkey

Roast beef

When people in the United States and Canada talk about "sandwiches," they think of two pieces of bread with something in the middle – cheese, meat, or vegetables. However, cultures around the world use bread – or something like it – to make delicious meals you can hold in your hand. In Mexico, people eat tacos, flat tortillas wrapped around meat and vegetables. People in southern Asia (India, Pakistan) fill many kinds of breads with spicy curries. In the Middle East, people eat pita or pocket bread full of vegetables. Are sandwiches popular in your country? What kind?

LISTENING TASK 2
What's cooking?

Identifying a sequence

☐ Listen. Some students are learning how to make jambalaya, a dish from the southern part of the United States.

Put the pictures in order (1–9).

Shrimp Jambalaya

Ingredients:

1 piece of beef (chopped)
2 tablespoons butter
1 large onion
1/4 cup celery
1 green pepper
2 large tomatoes
2 cloves garlic
2 cups chicken broth
2 cups shrimp
2 cups of rice (uncooked)

Spices:
chili powder
white pepper
black pepper
cayenne pepper
Tabasco sauce
salt

3

9

1

7

2

6

4

5

8

YOUR TURN TO TALK

On another piece of paper, write one food for each:

1. a kind of sandwich   4. a vegetable you like   7. seafood
2. a fruit you like   5. a kind of salad   8. a food you don't like
3. a dessert   6. a drink   9. a kind of meat

Now, work in groups of three. Find out what foods your classmates wrote. How many people wrote the same thing?

Sample questions

What kind of sandwich did you write?   What did you write for number 2?

14

Listening Task 2 What's cooking?

Listening skill: Identifying a sequence

1. T: *Look at page 14.*

2. (**Optional**) Read the title: *"What's cooking?" What do you think this will be about?* Elicit answers from the students. (Answer: how to make a kind of food)

3. (**Optional**) If students find listening very difficult, do the Additional Support procedure below.

4. Play the instructions: *Listen. Some students are learning how to make jambalaya, a dish from the southern part of the United States. Put the pictures in order.*

5. Play Listening Task 2 on the tape. Gesture for students to write the numbers.

6. (**Optional**) To make sure students understand what to do, stop after two steps. Draw nine squares on the board in the pattern of the pictures. Ask students: *Which picture is first? Which is second?* Write the numbers in the correct squares. Then play the rest of Listening Task 2.

7. If necessary, play Listening Task 2 a second time. Before replaying the tape, you may want to have students compare their answers in pairs: *Work with a partner. Look at your partner's answers. How many were the same? Then we'll listen again.*

8. Check students' answers by drawing nine squares on the board. Have students identify the order as you write the numbers. It may be useful to write the words "top," "bottom," "middle," "left," and "right" on the board to help them identify the squares. (Answers appear in blue on the opposite page.)

ADDITIONAL SUPPORT Tell students they are going to learn how to make a food called jambalaya. Have them look at the recipe card. Answer questions about vocabulary. Have students work in pairs. Tell them to look at the pictures. On or next to each picture they should write one verb and at least one noun. They can refer to the cooking verbs on page 12.

NOTES

• The situation is a cooking class. Jambalaya was used as an example because most students do not know how to make it. Therefore, they have a reason for listening. Jambalaya is a Cajun food, popular with the French-speaking people in the state of Louisiana.

• Sequence markers like "first," "next," and "after that" are important to understanding this task. Students will have gotten some practice with these words in the Warming Up activity on page 12.

• The "up" in "cut up" is used to emphasize completion.

Your turn to talk

1. To begin, have students work alone. T: *On another piece of paper, write one food for each: (1) a kind of sandwich, (2) a fruit you like, (3) a dessert, (4) a vegetable you like, (5) a kind of salad, (6) a drink, (7) seafood, (8) a food you don't like, (9) a kind of meat.*

2. T: *Now work in groups of three. Find out what foods your classmates wrote. How many people wrote the same thing? (You get one point each time you and someone else wrote down the same food. You get two points if everyone wrote the same thing.)*

3. If you wish to do this activity as a game, there can be two winners: The team with the most total points has the most universal taste. The team with the lowest point total has the most individual taste.

UNIT 4
Gestures

Topic/function: Describing gestures in different countries
Listening skills: Understanding cultural information (Listening Task 1), understanding cultural differences (Listening Task 2)
Grammar/vocabulary: Parts of the body, verbs of motion

Warming Up

1. Hold your book so that students can see page 15. T: *Look at page 15.*

2. Read the instructions:

Gestures are actions you do with your hands or head. They have different meanings in different cultures.

Work with a partner. Look at these gestures from the United States and Canada.

Are there gestures for these meanings in your country?

Do the gestures.

3. (**Optional**) Do the gestures illustrated and say the words "goodbye," "yes," etc. As you say the words, have students do gestures with the same meaning for their own culture(s).

4. Read the rest of the instructions: *What other gestures do you use? Write the meanings.* As students work, circulate and help pairs having difficulty. If students are having difficulty thinking of other gestures, do one or two and have them say the English meaning. Possible gestures are listed in Notes.

5. Check by having pairs do their gestures and having other students say the meanings.

NOTES

• Students may need some help in thinking of gestures. Be prepared to perform a few. Some of the most common gestures are used to indicate *yes, no, I don't know, and me.* Common classroom gestures include *listen, quiet,* and *stop.*

Strategy exercise: *Visualizing*

Having students image themselves doing an action can help them remember the action and related vocabulary. Begin by demonstrating a series of gestures. They can be either gestures associated with English or gestures from the students' native language(s) along with the meaning in English. Demonstrate each gesture two or three times as you say the meaning. Then have students close their eyes. Slowly repeat the words. Tell students to imagine themselves doing the actions.

Optional activity

(For use anytime during or after the unit.)

• *Body language.* Gestures are one aspect of body language. Others include eye contact, physical distance between speakers, and understanding. To encourage students' awareness of these factors, have them work first in groups of about four. They list as many "rules" as they can. After 2 or 3 minutes, the groups break up. Everyone finds a new partner from a different group. They have a short conversation about a given topic, for example, what they did the previous weekend. As they speak, they break one of the rules (stand too close, avoid eye contact, etc.). The partner tries to decide which rule was broken.

Gestures

WARMING UP

Gestures are actions you do with your hands or head.
They have different meanings in different cultures.

❑ Work with a partner.
   Look at these gestures from the United States and Canada.
   Are there gestures for these meanings in your country?
   Do the gestures.

Goodbye.

Yes.

Money!

I'm surprised.

Come here.

❑ What other gestures do you use?
   Write the meanings.

_____

_____

_____

_____

1. In most countries . . .
a *nod* means

☑ yes.
☐ no.   *Greece*

2. In Tonga . . .
raised eyebrows mean

☑ yes.
☐ money.   *Peru*

3. In Argentina . . .
tapping your head means

☐ that person's crazy!   *Canada*
☑ I'm thinking.

4. In the Netherlands . . .
tapping your elbow means

☐ that person doesn't want to
spend money.   *Colombia*
☑ you can't depend on that person.

LISTENING TASK 1

What does that mean?

One person in each conversation above uses a gesture.
The first speaker is on the left.

❏ Listen. What do the gestures mean in these places?
Check (✔) the correct meaning (1–8).

 CULTURE CORNER Sometimes the same gesture can have very different meanings in different cultures. For example, in the United States and Canada, it is common to make a circle with your thumb and first finger. It means "OK." In Japan, the same sign means "money." In southern France, it stands for "zero" or "worthless." Be careful! If you travel to Brazil or Greece, do not use this sign. It has a very bad meaning. Are there gestures that you should not use in your country?

Listening Task 1
What does that mean?

Listening skill: Understanding cultural information

Note: The tapescript for Unit 4 begins on page T6.

1. T: *Look at pages 16 and 17.*

2. (**Optional**) Read the title: *"What does that mean?" What do you think this activity will be about?* Elicit answers from the students. (Answer: the meaning of gestures)

3. (**Optional**) If students find listening very difficult, do the Additional Support procedure below.

4. Read the instructions: *One person in each conversation above uses a gesture. The first speaker is on the left. Listen. What do the gestures mean in these places? Check the correct meaning.*

5. Play Listening Task 1 on the tape. Gesture for students to write their answers.

6. (**Optional**) To make sure students understand what to do, stop after two items. Do the gestures as you ask: *In (place), what does this mean?* Encourage students to answer. When they do, check the answer in your book.

7. If necessary, play Listening Task 2 a second time.

8. Check by eliciting answers from the class. (Answers appear in blue on pages 16 and 17.)

ADDITIONAL SUPPORT Have students work in pairs or groups of three. They look at all eight illustrations on both pages. They read the meanings for each gesture. If one of the meanings is the same in their own culture(s), they circle it. If the gesture has a different meaning to them, they write the meaning. If it has no meaning in their own culture, they don't do anything. This activity will make students more aware of the information they are listening for.

NOTES

• These gestures are presented as interesting examples. Students should understand that gestures and body language are important in speaking any language. However, students need not know or practice these particular gestures.

• The main sources of information for this unit were *Do's and Taboos Around the World*, 2nd edition (1990) and *Gestures* (1991), both by Roger E. Axtell, New York: John Wiley and Sons.

Culture corner

1. After they have read the Culture Corner, you may want to have students compare their answers to the question: *Are there gestures that you should not use in your country?* You might want students to just show the gesture and say individually "Don't do this."

2. (**Optional**) Before they read the Culture Corner, have students work in groups of three. One student is the reader. That student looks at page 16. The others open their books to the world map on pages 66 and 67. Tell students they will race to touch the countries mentioned. If the gesture has a good meaning, they must touch the country with their right hand. If the meaning is bad, they touch it with their left hand. The student looking at page 16 reads the passage aloud as the partners listen and touch the countries. Then they all go back and read the passage silently.

Listening Task 2
It's different there.

Listening skill: Understanding cultural differences

1. T: *Look at pages 16 and 17 again.*

2. (**Optional**) Read the title: *"It's different there." What do you think this activity will be about?* Elicit answers from the students. (Answer: different meanings for the same gestures)

3. (**Optional**) If students find listening very difficult, do the Additional Support procedure below.

4. Read the instructions: *Listen. In some places, the gestures have a different meaning. Write the names of the countries next to the meanings.*

5. Play Listening Task 2 on the tape. Gesture for students to write the names of the countries.

6. (**Optional**) To make sure students understand what to do, stop after the first two items. Ask students: *Where does raised eyebrows mean "money"?* (Answer: Peru) Then play the rest of Listening Task 2.

7. If necessary, play Listening Task 2 a second time. Before replaying the tape, you may want to have students compare their answers in pairs: *Work with a partner. Look at your partner's answers. How many were the same? Then we'll listen again.*

8. Check by asking the questions (*Where does _____ mean _____?*) and encouraging the students to answer. (Answers appear in blue on pages 16 and 17.)

ADDITIONAL SUPPORT The meanings not used in Listening Task 1 are mentioned in this task. Have students look at these meanings. Play the tape once. When students hear the meaning or the gesture mentioned, have them indicate it either by touching the picture or by doing the gesture itself.

NOTES
• You may prefer to check students' answers after each segment rather than waiting until students have heard all eight parts.

Your turn to talk

1. Divide the class into groups of three. T: *Work in groups of three. How many gestures can you think of? Write at least 15.* As they write, circulate and help. If students have difficulty thinking of 15 gestures, have them look through the unit and think of gestures they know that mean the things listed.

2. T: *Now think of a story. Your story should include at least eight of the gestures. Practice pantomiming the story.* Help groups that are having difficulty. Remind them that nearly any story has some kind of a problem. If they think of the problem first, it becomes easier to think of the story.

3. (after a few minutes) Have one student in each group join another group and pantomime the story to the new group. The group guesses the meaning.

Variation: After groups have made the list of gestures in step 1, have them exchange lists. They make their stories based on someone else's list.

A popular theme for student-generated stories in this activity is cross-cultural miscommunication.

Optional activity
(For use anytime during or after the unit.)

• *Gestures in our country.* Have students work in groups to answer the following questions: What gestures does your mother make? Your father? Your friends? You? Students should explain the meanings of the gestures.

5. In most parts of Europe . . .
circling your head means

- ☑ that person's crazy.
- ☐ there's a telephone call. *the Netherlands*

6. In Italy . . .
flicking your chin means

- ☐ I don't know. *Brazil*
- ☑ go away!

7. In the United States . . .
thumbs up means

- ☐ something bad. *Nigeria*
- ☑ everything is OK.

8. In Germany . . .
tossing your head means

- ☐ no. *Italy*
- ☐ yes. *India*
- ☑ come here.

LISTENING TASK 2

It's different there.

- ❏ Listen. In some places, the gestures have a different meaning.
  Write the names of the countries next to the meanings (1–8).
  Use these countries:

Brazil	Canada	Colombia	Greece
India	Italy	the Netherlands	Nigeria
Peru	Spain	Taiwan	

YOUR TURN TO TALK

Work in groups of three. How many gestures can you think of? Write at least 15. Then think of a story. Your story should include at least eight of the gestures. Practice pantomiming the story. Then pantomime it to another group. They will try to guess the story.

Didn't you see that sign?

Signs should be easy to understand.
These aren't.

❏ Work with a partner.
Look at the signs.
What do you think they mean?

1.

2.

3.

4.

❏ Check your answers at the bottom of page 20.

U N I T 5
Didn't you see that sign?

Topics/functions: Stating rules and giving
   permission
Listening skills: Inferring meaning of signs
   (Listening Task 1), understanding rules
   (Listening Task 2)
Grammar/vocabulary: Modals: *can* and
   should

Warming Up

1. Hold your book so that students can see
page 18. T: *Look at page 18.*

2. Read the following instructions (or play
the instructions on the tape).

   *Signs should be easy to understand. These
      aren't.*
   Work with a partner. Look at the signs.
   What do you think they mean?

3. Demonstrate by eliciting suggestions
from two or three students: *What do you
think number 1 means?* Gesture for them to
write their answers.

4. As students work, circulate and help
pairs having difficulty. Make sure students
realize that this is a guessing game. They
aren't expected to be sure about the
meaning of each sign. They should guess.

5. T: *After you've guessed, check your answers
at the bottom of page 20.*

NOTE

• These signs introduce the idea that
signs are not always as clear as their makers
think they are. Students will have to guess
the meaning of other signs in Listening
Task 1. Students should be encouraged to
guess; they should not feel they have to get
the right answer.

Strategy exercise: Associating

People learn by associating new
information with old. Often, students are
not as successful as they could be because
they see English as a random collection of
rules and words. Divide students into
groups of four or five. Give all groups the
same word–one they are all familiar
with–and set a time limit. One student in
each group is the secretary. The groups
race against each other to list as many
words as they can that are associated with
the word given. The group with the most
associations wins. After they understand
the task, have groups try the game with
some new words in this unit. "Rules" or
"recreation" may be appropriate words to
use the first time you do this. Possible new
vocabulary: "exercise," "earthquake,"
"historic," "chemicals," and "ranger."

Optional activities

(For use anytime during or after the unit.)

• ***Rules we need.*** Have students working in
small groups (three to five students) think
of rules or laws that would improve their
city or school. What should people stop
doing? What should they do more often?
What should happen if people break the
rules?

• ***Making a sign.*** Have students working in
groups of three think of a rule that many
people break (for example, parking in the
wrong place). The group should think of
an easy-to-understand sign and draw it.
The groups should try to guess the
meaning of each other's signs.

Listening Task I
What do they really mean?

> **Listening skill:** Inferring meaning of signs

Note: The tapescript for Unit 5 begins on page T8.

I. T: *Look at page 19.*

2. (**Optional**) Read the title: *"What do they really mean?" What do you think this will be about?* Elicit answers from the students. (Answer: the meaning of these signs)

3. Read the first part of the instructions: *What do you think these signs mean? Check the correct box.* Stop the tape to give students time to mark their answers.

4. (**Optional**) If students find listening very difficult, do the Additional Support procedure below.

5. Read the rest of the instructions and Listening Task 1 on the tape: *Now listen. What do the signs mean? Circle the answers.* Gesture for students to circle the answers.

6. (**Optional**) To make sure students understand what to do, stop after two items. Ask two or three students: *What does number two mean?* Then play the rest of Listening Task 1.

7. If necessary, play Listening Task 1 a second time.

8. Check by having students call out their answers. (Answers appear in blue on the opposite page.)

ADDITIONAL SUPPORT Have students do steps 3 and 5 above in pairs.

NOTES

• This is an inference activity. The exact words under the signs aren't used. Students get the meaning based on what is said.

• You may prefer to check students' answers after each segment rather than waiting until students have heard all eight parts. If you do, ask students how they knew the answers. This will allow students to hear the "inference clues" their classmates used.

• As with the Warming Up activity, the meanings of the signs in Listening Task 1 are unclear. This is to add interest and challenge to the task. Students shouldn't feel that they should know the meaning of the signs before they hear the tape.

• The phrase "point of interest" is generally used on signs and in guide books, not in conversation.

Culture corner

I. After they have read the Culture Corner, you might want students in small groups to compare their answers to the question: *What unusual laws do you have in your country?*

2. (**Optional**) This Culture Corner contains several words that may be new to students ("fines," "flushing," "register," etc). Have students read the Culture Corner without using their dictionaries. In pairs, have them guess the meaning of any unfamiliar words. They should base their guesses on the rest of the information in the paragraph. They may need to guess in their native language(s). Finally, have them check their dictionaries to see if they were correct.

What do they really mean?

❑ What do you think these signs mean?
Check (✔) the correct box.

❑ Now listen. What *do* the signs mean?
Circle the answers.

1.
   ❑ Recreation/exercise area
   ❑ (Do not enter.)

2.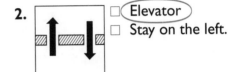
   ❑ (Elevator)
   ❑ Stay on the left.

3. ❑ You can turn your car around.
   ❑ (Point of interest)

4.
   ❑ Lock your car.
   ❑ (Rent a car)

5. ❑ Earthquake area
   ❑ (Unusual nature site)

6.
   ❑ (Old building)
   ❑ Chemicals

7.
   ❑ (The water is deep.)
   ❑ No swimming.

8.
   ❑ (Meeting place)
   ❑ Crossroad

Many countries have laws which surprise visitors from abroad. People may have to pay fines – money – because they have broken a law. For example, the fine for chewing gum at the Statue of Liberty in New York City is $250. In Singapore, there is a fine for not flushing the toilet. Also in Singapore, monkeys must have identification cards. Their owners must register them. In Malaysia, you can't wear a motorcycle helmet that covers your face. What unusual laws do you have in your country?

CULTURE CORNER

LISTENING TASK 2

You can't do that.

Rangers work in parks and campgrounds.
They take care of the park and make sure people are safe.

❑ Listen. A ranger is explaining the park rules.
Some things in the picture are against the rules.
Cross out (**X**) the activities that are against the rules.

YOUR TURN TO TALK

There are many kinds of rules: laws (the speed limit when driving, where you can and can't smoke), school rules ("You must come to class," "You have to do homework"), personal rules ("I always do my homework before I watch TV"), rules of right and wrong ("Don't lie"). Work in groups of five. What laws and school rules do you have to follow? What are your personal rules and rules of right and wrong? Write as many rules as you can in five minutes. Have you broken any of these rules? Which ones? Why?

Meanings of signs on page 18: 1. There is a public telephone. 2. You must keep to the right. 3. Customs. You must have your baggage checked. 4. Up escalator.

Listening Task 2
You can't do that.

Note: You may wish to prepare an overhead projector (OHP) transparency of the illustration to use when correcting this task.

1. T: *Look at page 20.*

2. (**Optional**) Read the title: *"You can't do that." What do you think this will be about?* Elicit answers from the students. (Answer: rules)

3. (**Optional**) If students find listening very difficult, do the Additional Support procedure.

4. Read the instructions: *Rangers work in parks and campgrounds. They take care of the park and make sure people are safe. Listen. A ranger is explaining the park rules. Some things in the picture are against the rules. Cross out the activities that are against the rules.*

5. Play Listening Task 2 on the tape. Gesture for students to cross out the things that aren't allowed.

6. (**Optional**) To make sure students understand what to do, stop after the first two items. Ask: *What is against the rules?* (Answers: open fires, cutting firewood) Then play the rest of Listening Task 2.

7. If necessary, play Listening Task 2 a second time. Before playing the tape, you may want to have students compare their answers in pairs: *Work with a partner. Look at your partner's answers. How many were the same? Then we'll listen again.*

8. Check answers by having students say what was against the rules. You may wish to point to them on an OHP. (Answers appear in blue on the opposite page.)

ADDITIONAL SUPPORT Have students work in pairs. They circle things they think might be against the park rules. An alternative is to have students close their books. They brainstorm park rules in their own country (countries). List them on the board.

NOTES

• The ranger is being quite direct because it is important that the rules be followed. In conversation, you probably would not say "don't . . ." or "you cannot . . . ," but in this situation it is quite appropriate because the ranger is in a position of authority.

• "Firepits" are places to build fires, usually surrounded by rocks; an "open fire" is one built in the open, not in a special place.

Your turn to talk

1. T: *What kinds of rules do you have to follow?* Elicit types of rules [laws, school/work rules, personal rules, moral/religious rules (right and wrong), etc.]. Write the types on the board. If students volunteer a specific rule rather than a type (e.g., "We must have a license to drive"), restate the rule along with its type (e.g., "We have to have a license to drive" is a law).

2. T: *Work in groups of five. What rules do you have to follow? How many can you write in five minutes?*

3. (after about 5 minutes) T: *Have you broken any of these rules? Which ones? Why?* Allow time for students to talk about the rules in their groups.

Note: If marking pens and large pieces of paper are available, you may want to use them for step 2. The large print of markers makes it easier for groups to compare lists if they wish to.

Variation: Students make a list of rules they follow in daily life that they like, that they don't like, that are useful, and that are not useful.

How do you feel?

Topic/function: Discussing health and
  habits
Listening skills: Identifying behavior
  (Listening Task 1), understanding
  suggestions (Listening Task 2)
Grammar/vocabulary: simple present,
  imperatives

Warming Up

1. Hold your book so that students can see
page 21. T: *Look at page 21. This is a health
survey.*

2. Read the following instructions. Pause
when you see the symbol ♦ to give
students time to answer the questions.

> *Work with a partner.*
> *Ask the questions in the survey.*
> *Check the answers for your partner.* ♦

3. Demonstrate how the survey is done by
selecting one pair. As the other students
watch, gesture for one student to ask the
first question ("Do you smoke?"). When
the partner answers, gesture for the first
student to mark the answer in his or her
book.

4. As students work, circulate and help
pairs having difficulty.

5. When students have finished, have
them find their partners' score: *Add up
your partner's score. Add one point for each
"yes" answer to questions 2 and 5. Add one
point for each "no" answer to questions 1, 3, 4,
6, 7, and 8.*

NOTE

• Questionnaires like this can be found in
newspapers and magazines. These
questionnaires are very popular and are
often used to address serious issues (like
health) in an entertaining way.

Strategy exercise: *Using the body as well as
the mind*

One way to learn new words is to act them
out. The motion is another clue to
remembering the word. Divide the class
into an even number of small groups. Each
group looks through the unit and selects
four or five new, unusual, or difficult
words. Then sets of two groups work
together. One group acts out the words
selected while members of the other group
try to guess the words. Words likely to be
included are *"exercise," "stress," "checkup,"*
and *"confidence."*

Optional activities

(For use anytime during or after the unit.)

• *Find someone who . . .* Write the
following on the chalkboard:

> Find somone who. . .
>   1. sleeps fewer than 5 hours a night
>   2. sleeps more than 10 hours a night
>   3. exercises every day
>   4. never exercises
>   5. wants to move to a bigger city
>   6. wants to move to a smaller city

Students should all stand up and try to
find classmates that answered "yes" to the
questions. If they find someone who said
"yes," they should write that person's
name; then they must ask someone else.
They may not write the same person's
name more than once.

• *Opposites.* Students work in groups of
four and look at page 22. They should find
the things they should not do, then think
of reasons why people might like to do
those things. They should then find the
healthy things and think of reasons why
people might not do them.

How do you feel?

❏ Work with a partner.
Ask the questions in the survey.
Check (✔) the answers for your partner.

☤ Health Notes

How Healthy Are You?

	Yes	No
1. Do you smoke?	❏	❏
2. Do you have a checkup at your doctor's office once a year?	❏	❏
3. Do you sleep more than 10 hours a day?	❏	❏
4. Do you sleep less than 5 hours a day?	❏	❏
5. Do you exercise (cycling, walking, swimming, dancing, etc.) more than 20 minutes at least three times a week?	❏	❏
6. Do you live in a city?	❏	❏
7. Do you work more than 10 hours a day?	❏	❏
8. Is your life stressful?	❏	❏

❏ Add up your partner's score.
Add one point for each "yes" answer to
questions 2 and 5.
Add one point for each "no" answer to
questions 1, 3, 4, 6, 7, and 8.

Partner's score _____
6–8 points = You're probably healthy.
3–5 points = You could do better.
0–2 points = Be careful!

I really should be more careful.

❏ Listen. Two friends are talking about health.
Do they do these things? Write "yes" or "no."

 **June**　　 **Andy**

		June	Andy
	1. smoke	no	yes
	2. visit the doctor	yes	no
	3. sleep too much	no	no
	4. sleep too little	no	no
	5. exercise	no	no
	6. live in a city	yes	yes
	7. work too much	no	yes
	8. have a lot of stress	yes	yes

CULTURE CORNER

Exercise is an important part of staying healthy. In the United States and Canada, the most popular ways to exercise include walking (22% of Americans and Canadians walk for exercise), swimming (17%), bicycling (13%), running/jogging (11%), and playing tennis (9%). Staying healthy isn't the only reason people exercise. Other reasons are:

to feel better	80%	to reduce stress	62%
to look better	48%	to have more confidence	33%

Do you exercise? What kinds of exercise are popular in your country?

Listening Task 1
I really should be more careful.

Listening skill: Identifying behavior

Note: The tapescripts for Unit 6 begin on page T9.

1. T: *Look at page 22.*

2. (**Optional**) Read the title: *"I really should be more careful." What do you think this activity will be about?* Elicit answers from the students. (Answers: health and the health survey on the previous page)

3. (**Optional**) If students find listening very difficult, do the Additional Support procedure below.

4. Read the instructions: *Listen. Two friends are talking about health. Do they do these things? Write "yes" or "no."*

5. Play Listening Task 1 on the tape. Gesture for students to write their answers.

6. (**Optional**) To make sure students understand what to do, stop after one or two items. Focus their attention on the page: Does June visit the doctor? (Answer: yes). Does Andy visit the doctor? (Answer: no). Then play the rest of Listening Task 1.

7. If necessary, play Listening Task 1 a second time.

8. Check by reading each item and having students raise their hands for "yes" and "no." *Does June smoke? Yes?* (pause) *No?* Repeat the correct answers. (Answers appear in blue on the opposite page.)

ADDITIONAL SUPPORT Have students close their books. Then have them listen to Listening Task 1. As they listen, they should try to note any words or topics related to health.

NOTES

• One person has found a questionnaire on health in a newspaper. The friends are answering the questionnaire together.

• If your students are from countries where "yes" and "no" are sometimes symbolized with *O* and *X*, you can save time in step 8 by having them form circles and Xs with their arms. Students who answered "yes" and students who answered "no" can respond at the same time.

• Note the use of the present tense for habitual actions. Also note the use of *should* as both a way to offer suggestions to another person and to offer advice to oneself. (You really should slow down. Yes, I should relax more.)

Culture corner

1. After the students have read the Culture Corner, you might want to ask these questions: *Do you exercise? What kinds of exercise are popular in your country?*

2. (**Optional**) To see how answers from the class compare with the information about the United States and Canada, have students list the five types of exercise named. Each student then asks at least ten other students if they do these sports ("Do you walk for exercise?" "Do you swim?" etc.). Students find their own statistics. Finally, you may want to poll the whole class. Have students raise their hands for each exercise. Have them find the percentages for the class.

Listening Task 2 Stressed out

Listening skill: Understanding suggestions

1. T: *Look at page 23.*

2. (**Optional**) Read the title: *"Stressed out." What do you think this activity will be about?* Elicit answers from the students. (Answer: someone under too much stress/pressure)

3. (**Optional**) If students find listening very difficult, do the Additional Support procedure below.

4. Read the instructions: *Listen. Mia is feeling a lot of stress. Which things does her friend suggest? Check them. What does she say about each idea? Write one thing.*

5. Play Listening Task 2 on the tape. Gesture for students to mark their answers.

6. (**Optional**) To make sure students understand what to do, stop after the friend makes one or two suggestions. Ask students: *What did the friend suggest?* (Answer: exercise) *What else did she say?* (Answers: ride a bicycle, walk, go swimming) Then play the rest of Listening Task 2.

7. If necessary, play Listening Task 2 a second time. Before replaying the tape, you may want to have students compare their answers in pairs. T: *Work with a partner. Look at your partner's answers. How many were the same? Then we'll listen again.*

8. Check students' answers by asking which items students heard. Also ask what else they wrote. Write them on the board. (Answers appear in blue on the opposite page.)

ADDITIONAL SUPPORT Have students listen twice. The first time they only need to catch which items are mentioned. The second time they try to understand extra information.

NOTES

• "Stressed out" is an idiom. It means to suffer from too much pressure.

• The speakers are friends, so the advice is given very directly: "You need to manage that stress . . ." "You really should ride a bicycle . . ." Also, here the friend is urging Mia to get more exercise without becoming a "fitness nut." The phrase "fitness nut" is an expression meaning "someone who is always exercising." It would be considered impolite to call someone you didn't know very well a fitness nut.

Your turn to talk

1. Divide the class into groups of four. T: *Work in groups of four. What do people in your group do to stay healthy? How many different things have people done in the past week? List them.*

2. Demonstrate by having several people give answers. Gesture for them to write their answers.

3. (after about 5 minutes) T: *How many did your group write?*

4. (**Optional**) Have one group read out their list. Other groups who wrote the same items raise their hands. Continue this way with other groups.

LISTENING TASK 2

Stressed out

❏ Listen. Mia is feeling a lot of stress.
Which things does her friend suggest? Check (✔) them.
What does she say about each idea? Write one thing.

✔ **exercise**
ride a bicycle / walk / go swimming

☐ see a doctor
_____

✔ **learn yoga**
helps you relax

☐ change your job
_____

✔ **have more fun**
see a movie

✔ **take vitamins**
take them every day

YOUR TURN TO TALK

Work in groups of four. What do people in your group do to stay healthy? How many different things have people done in the past week? List them. In your class, which group can list the most items? What are the most popular ways to stay healthy?

Where is it?

❑ Work with a partner.
Think of places in your town or area.
Don't say the names of the places.
Give directions to the places.
Start at a well-known building.

Partner, follow the directions. Guess the places.
What are the places? Write them.

_____

_____

_____

Go past the bank.

Turn right at the hospital.

Go straight three blocks.

It's on the southwest corner.

Turn left at the
second traffic light.

YOU ARE HERE
×

Drawing by Chas. Addams; © 1974
The New Yorker Magazine, Inc.

UNIT 7
Where is it?

Warming Up

1. Hold your book so that students can see
page 24. T: *Look at page 24.*

2. (Optional) Read the direction
sentences (*Go past the bank*, etc.) to the
students and have them repeat them.

3. Read the instructions:

Work with a partner.
Think of places in your town or area.
Don't say the names of the places.
Give directions to the places.
Start at a well-known building.
Partner, follow the directions.
Guess the places.
What are the places? Write them.

4. Demonstrate by giving an example:

Start at _____.
Go east *three blocks.*
Turn right. *(etc.)*

Encourage students to guess the place.

5. As students work, circulate and help
pairs having difficulty. Check the
understanding of those pairs by
whispering to one of the students *Tell your
partner how to get to _____.* Listen and
help as that student gives directions.

NOTES

• The purpose of this activity is to get
students thinking about giving directions.
Focus on the accuracy of their language,
not on the accuracy of their directions.
Your town may have some features like
winding streets that present special
challenges to people who try to describe
them. This would be a good time to tell
students ways to do this in English.

• Directions are usually given in the
imperative (order) form. Imperatives
usually don't have a subject unless the
person spoken to is not clear.

• "Please" is not usually used when giving
instructions ("Please go down this
street."). This is because, in English,
"please" is used for things that help the
speaker ("Please tell me how to get there")
rather than for things that help the person
being spoken to.

Strategy exercise: *Focusing on specific words*

It is sometimes useful for students to
anticipate and listen for specific words that
are likely to contain the information they
need. Since students are listening to
locations and directions in this unit, have
them brainstorm prepositions (*in, next to,*
etc.) and other direction words (*right, left,
go straight,* etc.). Then have them listen to
the tape once with their books closed. Tell
them to note how many times they hear
each preposition and direction word. A
variation that can be used in Listening
Task 2 is for students to point to the left,
right, or straight as they listen. This adds a
physical component to the activity.

Optional activities
(For use anytime during or after the unit.)

• ***Places in this town.*** Students work in
pairs. They give directions to their homes
from the school while their partner draws
a map.

• ***Blindfold directions.*** Students work in
pairs or small groups. One student is
blindfolded and directed around the
room. You may want to rearrange the
furniture or place other obstacles in their
path.

Listening Task 1 The park

Note: The tapescript for Unit 7 begins on page T10.

1. T: *Look at page 25.*

2. (Optional) Read the title: *"The park." What do you think this activity will be about?* Elicit answers from the students. (Answer: locations of things in a park)

3. (Optional) If students find listening very difficult, do the Additional Support procedure below.

4. Hold your book so that students can see page 25. Point to the six items (the playground, the boat rental, etc.) at the top of the page. Read the instructions: *Listen. Where are these places? Write the numbers on the map.*

5. Play Listening Task 1 on the tape. Gesture for students to write their answers.

6. (Optional) To make sure students understand what to do, stop after the first two. Have all the students point to the space for the boat rental. Point to your book to confirm. Then play the rest of Listening Task 1.

7. If necessary, play Listening Task 1 a second time.

8. Check answers by having students call out the locations. Another way to check is by having students point to the places in their books. Always wait 2 or 3 seconds before pointing to the correct places in your book. (Answers appear in blue on the opposite page.)

ADDITIONAL SUPPORT Have students work in groups of three or four. With their books closed, they think of as many prepositions ("in," "on," "under") and prepositional phrases ("to the right," "in the middle") as they can. Then they write them on a large sheet of paper. Play the tape. Whenever students think they hear one of the items, they point to it. This not only gives them an additional chance to listen, it also allows group members to help each other spot the prepositions.

NOTES

• Students will hear many prepositions of location in this exercise. They will also hear "just (past)" and "right (before)." These words intensify the prepositions; the things are located immediately past or immediately before.

• Imperatives are used here to give directions e.g., "Turn right after the tennis courts." At other times, only the description of the place is given (e.g., "It's between the lake and the trees"). The speaker assumes that the listener knows where the lake and the trees are.

Culture corner

1. After students have read the Culture Corner, you may want them to compare in groups their answers to the question: *Are there places with unusual names in your country?*

2. (Optional) Before students read the Culture Corner, have them work in groups of three. One looks at page 25. The others put one copy of the book between them and open to the world map on pages 66 and 67. The student looking at page 25 reads the Culture Corner. The others listen. Whenever they hear a country mentioned, they race to touch the country first. Having them actually touch the countries in the same book makes it clear who is fastest.

LISTENING TASK 1

The park

❏ Listen. Where are these places? Write the numbers on the map.

1. the playground

2. the boat rental

3. a telephone booth

4. the hot dog stand

5. the beach

6. the zoo entrance

CULTURE CORNER

NORWAY 14MI
DENMARK 23MI
SWEDEN 25MI

Where in the world would you see this? You're 14 miles (23 km) from Norway. Sweden is only 25 miles (40 km) away, and Denmark is even closer – 23 miles (37 km). You might think the sign is in Northern Europe. But it also says you're 37 miles (60 km) from Mexico, 46 miles (74 km) from Peru, and only 94 miles (151 km) from China. Actually, this unusual sign is in Maine in the United States. The places on the sign aren't the countries and famous cities. They're names of towns in the area! Are there places with unusual names in your country?

LISTENING TASK 2

How do I get there?

The Hotel Lotte is in Seoul, Korea.
It is a large and busy hotel.

❑ Listen. Some guests are at the front desk.
They are asking for directions to these 5 places.
Follow the directions. Write the numbers on the map.

1. The Bank of Korea
2. The Jung-an Map Shop
3. The British Embassy
4. The National Museum
5. The Chongmyo Shrines

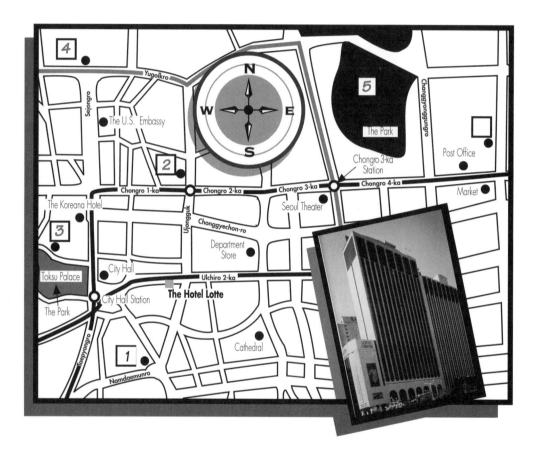

YOUR TURN TO TALK

Work with a partner. What are the five most interesting places for a visitor to your town or area? First list them. Explain why they're interesting. Then join another group. Combine your lists. Choose the three most interesting places. Think of directions for tourists. Start at the building you're in or another well-known place.

Example
A: How do you get to _____ ?
B: Well, walk out of the door and turn _____ . . .

Listening Task 2
How do I get there?

Listening skill: Following directions

1. T: *Look at page 26.*

2. (**Optional**) Read the title: *"How do I get there?" What do you think this activity will be about?* Elicit answers from the students. (Answer: giving directions in Seoul)

3. Read the instructions: *The Hotel Lotte is in Seoul, Korea. It is a large and busy hotel. Listen. Some guests are at the front desk. They are asking for directions to these 5 places. Follow the directions. Write the numbers on the map.*

4. Play Listening Task 2 on the tape. Gesture for students to follow the directions. (If students find listening very difficult, have them do this activity in pairs.)

5. (**Optional**) To make sure students understand what to do, stop after the second item on the tape. Tell the students: *Point to the Jung-an Map Shop.* After they do, point to it in your own book. Then play the rest of Listening Task 2.

6. If necessary, play Listening Task 2 a second time. Before replaying the tape, you may want to have students compare their answers in pairs. *Work with a partner. Look at your partner's answers. How many were the same? Then we'll listen again.*

7. Check by having students say the answers. You may wish to point to the places on an OHP transparency. Another way to check is to replay all of Listening Task 2. As you do, follow the directions with your finger on an OHP copy of the map. Students watch and check. (Answers appear in blue on the opposite page.)

ADDITIONAL SUPPORT Have students do step 4 in pairs. Pairs can also take turns thinking of a place on the map and giving directions from the Hotel Lotte to that place. Partners follow the directions.

NOTES

• The Hotel Lotte (pronounced *lō tay*) is one of Korea's most famous luxury hotels.

• You might have to teach the word "shrines" (a religious place or building).

• You may prefer to check students' answers after each segment rather than waiting until students have heard all five parts.

• If you have students who are Korean and very familiar with Seoul, you may want them to listen with their books closed to provide an additional challenge.

• The shapes of letters are sometimes used in English to describe street intersections. For example, number 4 on the tape uses "T-junction" in the directions to the National Museum. A T-junction is a spot where two streets cross in the shape of a capital (not a lowercase) "T." The letter "Y" is another example ("Go to the 'Y' in the road and then go left").

Your turn to talk

1. Divide the class into pairs. T: *What are the most interesting places in this area for tourists? List five. Why are they interesting? Now, work with a partner. Combine your lists. Decide on the three best places. How would you give directions?*

2. After about 5 minutes, you may want to poll the class to see how many pairs listed the same places.

U N I T   8
The world market

Topic/function: Discussing exports
Listening skills: Identifying origin
(Listening Task 1), following directions
(Listening Task 2)
Grammar/vocabulary: Adjectives of
nationality, prepositions of location,
modal: *should*

Warming Up

1. Hold your book so that students can see page 27. T: *Look at page 27.*

2. Read the instructions:

Exports are products that countries sell to other countries.

Sometimes exports are surprising. Work in groups of three.

Can you guess the biggest exports of the countries?

One person is game leader. Leader, look at page 70.

The others use this page. Play the game.

3. (**Optional**) To make sure all students understand, you may want to direct one group of three through the first couple of questions while the others watch.

4. As students work, circulate and help pairs having difficulty.

5. Check by asking the questions (*Which country's largest export is rice?* etc.). Students call out their answers and circle any answers that surprise them. This ensures that they both understand and think about the meaning.

NOTES

• The information is about the largest exports of the countries named. The countries may not be the world's largest exporters of these particular products.

• Data is from the *Information Please Almanac* (Houghton Mifflin, Boston, MA).

• The purpose of the Warming Up activity is to get students thinking about the topic. Some of the particular items may be surprising to most students. These were chosen to increase students' interest and motivation. There is no reason why learners should know the correct answers to the game, but by playing it, their interest in the unit topic is increased.

Strategy exercise: How will I remember?

After students have finished the unit, have them go through and circle any new words. Then have them work in pairs, trying to think of ways that could help them remember the words. They can use any images that help. For example, the terms "export" and "import" may be new. Students probably know that the word "port" is a place where ships bring products. *Im-* sounds like the word *in*. That may help students remember that imports are products coming into a country. *Ex-* often means "in the past." An *export* is a product that was here in the past but has been sent to another country. Likely new vocabulary in this unit includes "lumber," "chemical," "expo," and "nationality."

Optional activities

(For use anytime during or after the unit.)

• **How many countries?** Have students working in groups of about four look through everything they have with them (clothing, books, pencil cases, etc.) and try to find things made in as many countries as possible. They list the countries. Allow about 5 minutes. Then have students call out the countries. See how many countries they name.

• **International city.** Have students working in pairs think of all the connections between their city and the rest of the world. What things can be bought in their city that come from other countries? What places can be traveled to directly from that city? Which countries are people from?

The world market

WARMING UP

Exports are products that countries sell to other countries.
Sometimes exports are surprising.

❑ Work in groups of three.
Can you guess the biggest exports of the countries?
One person is game leader. Leader, look at page 70.
The others use this page. Play the game.

EXPORT CHALLENGE

Look at the products. Each product is the biggest export of one of these countries:

Australia	the Bahamas	Canada	China
France	India	Italy	Mexico
Norway	the Philippines	Spain	Thailand

Take turns. Guess the country which sells more of each product than any other product. (Cross out the country after a correct guess. There are two extra countries listed.)

PRODUCTS:

1. rice

2. beef

3. wheat

4. oil

5. cotton

6. clothing and cloth

7. fruit

8. diamonds

9. lobster

10. electronic equipment

Each correct answer = 1 point.
Your points: _____

World Trade Expo!

People are shopping at an international trade fair. Each country has a display.

❑ Listen. What countries are selling these products? Write the nationalities.

Brazilian	Canadian	French	German	Italian
Japanese	Korean	Spanish	Taiwanese	U.S.

1. leather shoes and bags
Spanish

2. cameras
Japanese

3. lumber and wood products
Canadian

4. computers
U.S.

5. watches
Taiwanese

6. TVs and video players
Korean

7. chemicals
German

8. coffee
Brazilian

CULTURE CORNER

International trade is important to nearly every country in the world. Sometimes it is difficult to really know where a product comes from. For example, 28 percent of Japanese cars sold in the United States are actually built in U.S. factories, not in Japan. Ten percent of cars from Chrysler – a large U.S. car company – are made in other countries. When companies send products to other countries, they need to think about many things, like prices, local styles, and taxes. Perhaps the most important thing to think about is quality. When people buy something expensive and like it, they usually tell eight other people. When they don't like it, they tell 22 others! What products does your country sell around the world?

Listening Task 1
World Trade Expo!

Listening skill: Identifying origin

Note: The tapescript for Unit 8 begins on page T12.

1. T: *Look at page 28.*

2. (**Optional**) Read the title: *"World Trade Expo!" What do you think this activity will be about?* Elicit answers from the students. (Answers: a trade fair, products from many countries)

3. (**Optional**) If students find listening very difficult, do the Additional Support procedure below.

4. Read the instructions: *People are shopping at an international trade fair. Each country has a display. Listen. What countries are selling these products? Write the nationalities* .

5. Play Listening Task 1 on the tape. Gesture for students to write their answers.

6. (**Optional**) To make sure students understand what to do, stop after one or two questions. Ask two or three students: *Where are the cameras from?* etc. Then play the rest of Listening Task 1.

7. If necessary, play Listening Task 1 a second time.

8. Check by having students call out their answers. (Answers appear in blue on the opposite page.)

ADDITIONAL SUPPORT In pairs, have students guess which countries will be mentioned for each product. They can base their guesses on the kinds of products they associate with the products listed. Although their guesses probably won't always be correct (most of the countries listed export many of the items), guessing the answers will make students more familiar with the information on the page.

It will also increase their interest when they listen to see if they were correct.

NOTES

• "Expo" is a short form of "exposition." Trade expos are also called trade fairs.

• To increase student interest, you may want to have students (working in pairs or small groups) guess what the answers will be before they listen. See the Additional Support procedure on this page.

• For many countries, the adjective (nationality) is the same as the word for a person from that country: Canadian wheat, a Canadian; Italian shoes, an Italian. Some exceptions are words ending in "sh" or "ch": English books, an Englishman/woman; French trains, a Frenchwoman/man.

• "Taiwanese" refers to products from Taiwan. Most people on the island are actually Chinese and prefer that term or "Taiwan–Chinese" when referring to themselves.

Culture corner

1. After students have read the Culture Corner, you may want to ask a few students to answer the question: *What products does your country sell around the world?*

2. (**Optional**) Before students read the Culture Corner, have them work in pairs with their books closed. Ask them to think about things they buy. What qualities do they think about? Price? Color? How fashionable it is? Each pair makes a list of at least six factors. Then they rank them from most important to least important. Finally, as they read the Culture Corner, they circle any factors they wrote that are also mentioned in the reading.

Listening Task 2
Where can I find that?

Listening skill: Following directions

1. T: *Look at page 29.*

2. (**Optional**) Read the title: *"Where can I find that?" What do you think this will be about? Elicit answers from the students.* (Answer: the locations of the things from Listening Task 1)

3. (**Optional**) If your students find listening very difficult, do the Additional Support procedure below.

4. Read the instructions: *Listen. The shoppers in Listening Task 1 are asking directions. Write the countries in the correct places.*

5. Play Listening Task 2 on the tape. Gesture for students to write the names of the countries on the page.

6. (**Optional**) To make sure students understand what to do, stop after the first two items. Ask: W*here is Japan's booth?* (Answer: at the end of the west wing) Point to your book to confirm. Then play the rest of Listening Task 2.

7. If necessary, play Listening Task 2 a second time. Before replaying the tape, you may want to have students compare their answers in pairs. *Work with a partner. Look at your partner's answers. How many were the same? Then we'll listen again.*

8. Check by asking students where each booth is located. As they answer, point to the correct spaces in your book. You may prefer to prepare an OHP transparency of the page or quickly draw the Expo Center on the board to make checking easier. (Answers appear in blue on the opposite page.)

ADDITIONAL SUPPORT Have students working in pairs look at the floor plan on page 29. One student thinks of one of the empty spaces and gives a hint ("It's next to the United Kingdom"). The partner asks a question to be sure of the place ("Is it across from the Netherlands?") and touches the space. Pairs continue for 3 or 4 minutes.

NOTES

• The taped items in the task are extensions of the conversations students heard in Listening Task 1.

• You may prefer to check students' answers after each segment rather than waiting until students have heard all eight parts.

• As used in this listening, a "wing" is a section of a building that stands out from the main or central part. Countries have "booths" or display areas in the wings of this Expo Center.

Your turn to talk

1. Divide the class into groups of 3. T: *Work in groups of three. You have seven minutes. How many countries and nationalities can you think of? What languages are spoken in these countries? Write them.*

2. (**Optional**) Elicit three or four examples.

3. (after 7 minutes) T: *Stop. How many did you list?*

4. (**Optional**) List all the countries on the chalkboard.

Variation: Instead of writing on paper, divide the students into teams. Have as many teams as possible write on the chalkboard at the same time. Give one piece of chalk to each team. When you say go, the first person on each team runs to the board and writes a country, nationality, and language. That person runs back and gives the chalk to the next person, who continues. At the end of the specified time, teams get one point for each item they listed plus a bonus point for any they listed that no other team did.

LISTENING TASK **2**

Where can I find that?

❏ Listen. The shoppers in Listening Task I are asking directions.
Write the countries in the correct places.

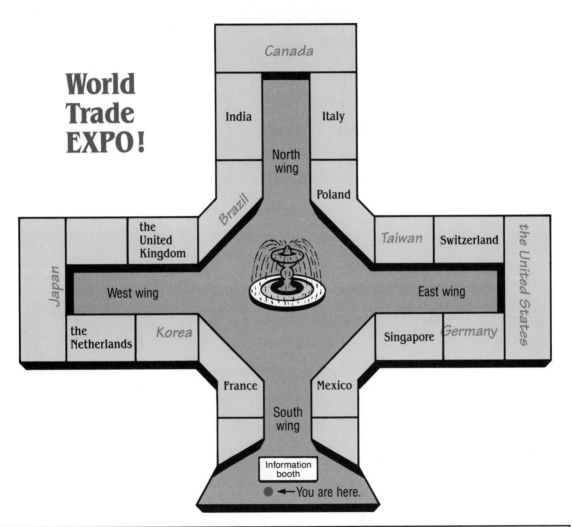

World Trade EXPO!

Canada

India | Italy

North wing

Brazil

Poland

the United Kingdom

Taiwan | Switzerland

Japan

West wing

the United States

East wing

the Netherlands | Korea

Singapore | Germany

France | Mexico

South wing

Information booth

● ←You are here.

YOUR TURN TO **TALK**

Work in groups of three. You have seven minutes. How many countries and nationalities can you think of? What languages are spoken in the countries? Which group could think of the most countries, nationalities, and languages?

Examples

Country	*Nationality*	*Language(s)*
Canada	Canadian	English, French
Brazil	Brazilian	Portuguese
Japan	Japanese	Japanese

What do they look like?

❏ Work in groups of three.
What words do you use to describe people?
Write at least two more words for each group below.

SAMPLE ANSWERS

1.

wavy — straight

hair

black — long

curly

2.

tall — heavy set

body type

thin — short

3.

brown eyes — glasses

face

round — chubby

What do they look like?

> **Topic/function:** Describing how people have changed
> **Listening skills:** Understanding physical descriptions (Listening Task 1), identifying differences (Listening Task 2)
> **Grammar/vocabulary:** Descriptive adjectives (people)

Warming Up

1. Hold your book so that students can see page 30. T: *Look at page 30.*

2. Read the instructions:

> *Work in groups of three.*
> *What words do you use to describe people?*
> *Write at least two more words for each group below.*

3. Do the first one as an example. Read the examples given. Write them on the board. T: *Hair can be wavy, straight, black. What else?* Encourage students to suggest other, related words (long, curly, parted, shoulder-length, blond, brown, etc.). T: *Do this with "body type" and "face."*

4. As students work, circulate and help pairs having difficulty. Encourage these pairs by pointing out the pictures at the bottom of the page, people in the room, or famous people with other physical characteristics. Ask questions such as: *What's his hair like?* If students don't know the English vocabulary, encourage them to ask "How do you say _____ in English?"

5. Check answers by encouraging students to say the words they wrote. Write them on the board.

NOTES

• Some students are reluctant to volunteer answers (as in step 5), especially in large classes. A technique to deal with

this is to have all students stand up. They can sit down once they've given an answer, even if the answer is wrong or if they say, "I don't know." No one will want to be the last person standing so students usually volunteer answers quickly. Stop the activity before there is only one person standing. This avoids the embarrassment of being called on and not knowing the answer.

• When using more than one adjective to describing people or objects, adjectives describe size or character come before color ("She has long black hair" not "She has black long hair").

Strategy exercise: Semantic mapping

This unit presents a strategy called "semantic mapping" in Warming Up. It helps students think about the words they are likely to hear in a listening passage, and it also helps them associate new words with old ones so that the words are better remembered. One way to help students practice this strategy is to have them work in pairs or small groups. Set a time limit (usually 3 to 5 minutes). Groups see how many words related to the topic they can list in the given time period. Other vocabulary areas related to describing people include clothing types and styles.

Optional activities

(For use anytime during or after the unit.)

• **Three changes.** Have students work in pairs. One person closes his or her eyes. The other changes three things about his or her appearance or clothing. The partner guesses the things that have changed.

• **Paired pictures.** Find pictures of people in magazines. Cut each picture in half. Give one half to each student. Students circulate throughout the room and try to find the second half of their picture by asking questions.

Listening Task 1
They've changed a little.

Note: The tapescript for Unit 9 begins on page T14.

1. T: *Look at page 31.*

2. (**Optional**) Read the title: *"They've changed a little." What do you think this activity will be about?* Elicit answers from the students. (Answer: changes in appearance over time)

3. Read the instructions: *Listen. Two friends are talking about these people. The people have changed since these pictures were taken. Circle what has changed.*

4. (**Optional**) If students find listening very difficult, do the Additional Support procedure below.

5. Play Listening Task 1 on the tape. Gesture for students to circle the changes.

6. (**Optional**) To make sure students understand what to do, stop after the description of the woman. Ask two or three students: *What's different about the woman?* Encourage them to answer (her hair is straight, she doesn't wear glasses). Then play the description of the man.

7. If necessary, play Listening Task 1 a second time.

8. Check by eliciting answers from the class. As students answer, gesture to make sure they understand the meaning of each item. (Answers appear in blue on the opposite page.)

ADDITIONAL SUPPORT Have students work in pairs or groups of three. They should look at the pictures and guess how the people's appearances might have changed. Each group makes at least one guess about each picture. Encourage the groups to call out their guesses as you write the key words on the board. This will ensure additional exposure to necessary vocabulary. Having made a guess, students are often more involved in the activity; they want to see if they are correct.

NOTES

• If your students had trouble thinking of descriptive adjectives in Warming Up, you might use magazine pictures and have them practice more before listening.

Culture corner

1. After students have read the Culture Corner, have them work in small groups to answer the questions: *What kind of descriptions have good meanings in your culture? Bad meanings?*

2. (**Optional**) After students have read the Culture Corner, have them work in groups of about four. Give them the following situations. (You may want to make copies or write these on the board.)

  a. someone has gained weight
  b. someone has lost weight
  c. someone has a new hairstyle
  d. someone has new clothing
  e. a man compliments a woman's appearance at work
  f. a woman compliments a man's appearance at work

Ask students if, in their own culture(s), it is OK to comment on these things. Is it common? When or where are these topics OK or not OK? Does the relationship of the speakers matter?

In North America, item (a) is almost never OK to talk about. Items (b) through (d) are usually OK as long as the comment is a compliment ("I like your new . . ."). The rules for items (e) and (f) (at work) are rather complicated and are changing. Generally, such compliments would be OK if made between friends. Normally, they wouldn't be made by a boss to an employee unless they are good friends.

They've changed a little.

❏ Listen. Two friends are talking about these people.
The people have changed since these pictures were taken.
Circle what has changed.

* hair: *straight and shorter*
* *contact lenses*

* *slimmer, especially face*
* *no mustache*

CULTURE CORNER

The way we describe people is sometimes based on culture. For example, in Thailand, when you tell a middle-aged man, "You look a little fat," it has a good meaning. It means, "You must be doing well and have a lot of food." In the United States and Canada, the meaning is bad: "You are eating too much and not taking care of yourself." What kind of descriptions have good meanings in your culture? Bad meanings?

31

LISTENING TASK 2

That's different!

❏ These pictures are not the same.
Look at the pictures for 30 seconds.
How many differences can you find? Circle them.

❏ Now listen. Circle the other differences.

The answers to this activity are listed on the facing page.

YOUR TURN TO TALK

Work with a partner. Look at your partner for exactly one minute. Try to remember everything about your partner's clothing and appearance. Then sit back-to-back so you can't see each other. Ask questions. See how much your partner remembers.

Sample questions
Do you remember what color my shirt is?
Do my shoes have laces?

Listening Task 2 That's different!

Listening skill: Identifying differences

1. T: *Look at page 32.*

2. Read the instructions: *These pictures are not the same. Look at the pictures for 30 seconds. How many differences can you find? Circle them.* Give the students exactly 30 seconds to try to find the differences.

3. Play Listening Task 2 on the tape. Gesture for students to circle the differences they hear.

4. If necessary, play Listening Task 2 a second time.

5. Check answers by having students call out the differences. As they do, point to them in your book or on an OHP transparency. (See Answers on this page.)

6. (**Optional**) If students find listening very difficult, do the Additional Support procedure.

ADDITIONAL SUPPORT If students are having difficulty, have them listen to the tape again after they have circled the correct answers. As you play the tape, point in your book or on an OHP transparency to the item talked about as it is mentioned. Students should watch your signals.

NOTES

• One item (the dog's eyes) is not mentioned. This allows students to know something not on the tape.

• Don't worry that your students will find all the differences without listening. They won't if you are strict about the 30-second time limit. The point is to get them to preview the material, to become interested, and to get an idea of where things are on the page so that they can do the task more easily.

ANSWERS

TOP PICTURE	BOTTOM PICTURE
The woman	
1. shoes	barefoot
2. glasses	no glasses
3. a belt	no belt
4. shoulder-length hair	shorter hair
The man	
5. gray shirt	white shirt
6. beard	no beard
7. straight hair	curly hair
8. thinner	heavier
The little girl	
9. lighter hair	darker hair
10. jeans	shorts
11. sunglasses	regular glasses
12. shorter	taller
The little boy	
13. black left eye	black right eye
14. short-lseeved shirt	ling-sleeved shirt
15. cap	no cap
The jogger	
16. T-shirt says USC	T-shirt says UBC
17. mustache	no mustache
18. smaller nose	bigger nose
19. more hair	less hair
The dog	
20. eyes open	eyes closed

Your turn to talk

1. Divide the class into pairs. T: *Work with a partner. Sit so you are facing each other. Look at your partner for exactly one minute. Try to remember everything about your partner's clothing and appearance.*

2. (after 1 minute) T: *Now sit back-to-back. Ask questions. Can your partner remember?*

Note: If your classroom has fixed seating, which makes it difficult for sitting back-to-back, have them do the activity standing up.

3. Direct one pair through the activity by pointing at the sample questions in the book. The partner answers. Let the game continue for about 5 minutes.

Variation: Have all the students close their eyes. Ask questions about your own appearance. The more specific the questions (*Is my watch gold or silver?*), the more interesting the activity becomes.

What do you do?

Topic/function: Talking about careers and future plans
Listening skills: Identifying/inferring occupations (Listening Task 1); understanding plans, inferring whether a situation is certain (Listening Task 2)
Grammar/vocabulary: Future with *going to*; future with *will*

Warming Up

1. Hold your book so that students can see page 33. T: *Look at page 33.* Read the following instructions. Pause when you see the symbol ♦ to give students time to answer the questions.

Look at the jobs.
Pick two that are similar in some way.
Draw a line between these jobs. For example, a chef and an artist.
The reason? They're both creative. ♦

2. T: *Pick four more pairs that are similar. Draw lines between them.* ♦

3. As they work, circulate and help students having difficulty. If many students are having trouble, do one or two examples as a full class. T: *How are a doctor and a lawyer the same?* (Sample answer: they both make a lot of money)

4. T: *Work with a partner. Look at your partner's pairs. Guess the way each pair is the same.*

5. Demonstrate this part of the activity by saying two jobs and having students guess. T: *A chef and a waiter or waitress.* (Answer: both work with food)

6. Gesture for the students to begin. As they work, circulate and help those having difficulty.

Strategy exercise: *New words in context*

Students often rely on their dictionaries too much. Dictionaries are useful, but like any tool, they need to be used correctly. Students shouldn't look up every new word they see or hear. One way to help them guess the meaning of a word is to give them a series of sentences. Each sentence gives a clue about the meaning. Students guess, usually in their native language(s), the meaning of the new words. For example, many students don't know the word "politician." Try reading the following clues for "politician" and have students guess the meaning.

Many politicians used to be lawyers.
In the United States, there are a lot of politicians in Washington, D.C.
The prime minister (or president) is a politician.
(Name of a famous politician) is a politician.

Do this with other words that may be new.

Optional activity

(For use anytime during or after the unit.)

• **Chalkboard race.** Divide students into teams. The number of teams should be determined by the space you have at your chalkboard. One member from each team will be writing at one time. The students line up. Give them a category: outside jobs, for example. The first member from each team goes to the board and writes an outside job, then returns and gives the chalk to the next team member, who goes to the board and writes another outside job. This continues until the board is filled or you stop the activity. The winning team is the one that has written the most jobs on the board. You can then change categories (jobs that need tools, for example) and repeat the activity.

What do you do?

WARMING **UP**

❑ Look at the jobs.
Pick two that are similar in some way.
Draw a line between these jobs.

Example

a chef ——————— *an artist*
The reason: They're both creative.

❑ Pick four more pairs that are similar.
Draw lines between them.

SAMPLE
ANSWERS

(They both work
in offices.)

a department
store clerk

a computer
programmer

a lawyer

a secretary

a bank teller

(They both
serve people.)

(They both give
speeches.)

(They're both
creative.)

an artist

a chef

(They both help
people.)

a police officer

VOTE

a politician

a businessperson

a doctor

❑ Work with a partner.
Look at your partner's pairs.
Guess the way each pair is the same.

33

Who are they talking to?

❏ Listen. Who are these people talking to?
Write the occupations on the line.
What words helped you know?
Write one or two words under each line.

1. *a waiter or waitress*

fish   vegetable   rice

2. *a teacher*

homework   report   book

3. *a secretary*

type   fax   file

4. *a doctor*

feeling fine   pain   hurt

5. *a bank teller*

traveler's checks   withdraw
savings account

6. *a police officer*

driving slower   ticket
lose license

CULTURE CORNER

The titles of some jobs are changing. The old names made the jobs sound as if they were only for men or only for women. The new names are the same for both males and females.

Old	New
airline stewardess/steward	flight attendant
fireman	fire fighter
mailman	letter carrier/post office clerk
policeman/woman	police officer
salesman/woman	sales clerk/sales representative

Have any jobs changed names in your country? What was the reason?

Listening Task 1
Who are they talking to?

Listening skill: Identifying/inferring occupations

Note: The tapescript for Unit 10 begins on page T15.

1. T: *Look at page 34.*

2. (**Optional**) Read the title: *"Who are they talking to?" What do you think this activity will be about?* Elicit answers from the students. (Answer: the occupations of the people being spoken to)

3. (**Optional**) If students find listening very difficult, do the Additional Support procedure below.

4. Read the instructions: *Listen. Who are the people talking to? Write the occupation on the line. What words helped you know? Write one or two words under each line.*

5. Play Listening Task 1 on the tape. Gesture for students to write their answers.

6. (**Optional**) To make sure students understand what to do, stop after the second item. Ask the class: What was the occupation? (Answer: teacher) Ask two or three students: *How did you know? What words told you?* Elicit answers (homework, report, book, etc.) Then play the rest of Listening Task 1.

7. If necessary, play Listening Task 1 a second time.

8. Check by eliciting answers from the students. (Sample answers appear in blue on the opposite page.) Most students will not get all the words listed. They only need to write one or two.

ADDITIONAL SUPPORT Write the following jobs on the board: *teacher, doctor, bank teller, computer programmer, police officer, store clerk, secretary, waiter/waitress.* As a class, brainstorm things associated with a teacher (books, homework, grades, chalk, etc.). In pairs, students think about three things associated with each job. Those things may not be included on the tape, but the activity will focus students' thinking and choices when they listen.

NOTES

• You may prefer to check answers after each segment rather than waiting until students have heard all six parts. Ask the follow-up questions (step 6) to allow students to hear the strategies and clues their classmates are using.

Culture corner

1. After students have read the Culture Corner, have them compare answers in pairs to these questions: *Have any jobs changed names in your country? Why?*

2. (**Optional**) To help students remember syllable stress, read the following words from the Culture Corner. Students listen and mark the stress.

Variation: Total Physical Response (TPR). Have students repeat the words, standing up on the stressed syllable. This activity can also be done in pairs or small groups if you make copies of the word list. One student in each pair or group reads the words.

    a. **fi**re fighter   e. **let**ter carrier
    b. **post** office clerk f. po**lice** officer
    c. **sales**clerk   g. sales repre**sen**tative
    d. **flight** attendant

Optional activity

(For use anytime during or after the unit.)

• *Jobs and tools.* On slips of paper, have the class write three occupations and three tools. (Jobs and tools should be written on separate pieces of paper, one tool for each job; for example, *carpenter, hammer.*) Collect the slips and redistribute them. Students circulate and try to find matches for jobs and tools: *Do you have a tool a carpenter uses? Do you have a job that uses a hammer?*

Listening Task 2
I'm going to become a programmer.

1. T: *Look at page 35.*

2. (**Optional**) Read the title: *"I'm going to become a programmer." What do you think this activity will be about?* Elicit answers from the students. (Answer: future occupations)

3. (**Optional**) If students find listening very difficult, do the Additional Support procedure below.

4. Read the instructions: *Listen. Some students are talking about jobs after graduation. What are they going to become? How sure are they? Check "yes," "maybe," or "no" for each profession.*

5. Play Listening Task 2 on the tape. Gesture for students to mark their answers.

6. (**Optional**) To make sure students understand what to do, stop after Kent's line, "teaching is different." Ask the students: *Is Kent going to become a teacher?* (Answer: no) Indicate that students should have checked "no." Then play the rest of Listening Task 2.

7. If necessary, play Listening Task 2 a second time. Before replaying the tape, you may want to have students compare their answers in pairs. *Work with a partner. Look at your partner's answers. How many were the same? Then we'll listen again.*

8. Check by eliciting answers from the class. (Answers appear in blue on the opposite page.)

ADDITIONAL SUPPORT Have students close their books. Write the following occupations on the board: *computer programmer, teacher, artist, lawyer, politician, chef, restaurant owner.* Students copy the list. Play the tape one time. Each time they hear a job mentioned, students make a mark next to it in their books. Don't expect them to catch every time each job is mentioned. The purpose of this activity is to give students a task while providing an additional opportunity to listen.

NOTES

- Diane wants to be a lawyer and then go into politics. Many U.S. politicians train as lawyers.

- Tony makes a distinction between a cooking school and a culinary school. "Culinary" implies instruction in how to cook food served in better restaurants.

- "Going to" and "will" are used a little differently to express future plans. "Going to" means a decision has been made and it is fairly certain (I'm going to be a teacher). "Will" is usually less certain (I'll be a teacher someday). Tone of voice can make "will" sound very certain (You don't believe me but I will be a teacher!). "Will" is also used at the time a decision is made (A: I'm going to the store. B: I'll come with you.).

Your turn to talk

1. Divide the class into groups of five. T: *Work in groups of five. Think of a job. Partners, ask yes-no questions about the job. When the answer is "yes," try to guess the job.*

2. (**Optional**) To prompt yes-no questions, write the following words on the board: *is, are, do, does, have.* T: *I'm thinking of a job. What is it?* Encourage students to ask yes-no questions. When someone gets a "yes" answer, encourage that student to guess the job: *What job do you think it is?*

3. T: *Take turns choosing different jobs.*

4. Allow students to play for 5 to 10 minutes. It is best to stop an activity before interest drops.

LISTENING TASK 2

I'm going to become a programmer.

❏ Listen. These students are talking about jobs after graduation.
What are they going to become? How sure are they?
Check "yes," "maybe," or "no" for each profession.

Maria	Kent	Diane	Tony

	Yes	**Maybe**	**No**
1. Maria a computer programmer	☑	☐	☐
2. Kent a teacher	☐	☐	☑
an artist	☐	☑	☐
3. Diane a lawyer	☑	☐	☐
a politician	☐	☑	☐
4. Tony a chef	☑	☐	☐
a restaurant owner	☑	☐	☐

YOUR TURN TO TALK

Work in groups of five. Think of a job. Partners, ask yes-no questions about the job.
When an answer is "yes," try to guess the job. Take turns choosing different jobs.

Example

Q: Is the job dangerous?   A: No.
Q: Do you make a lot of money?   A: Yes.
Q: Are you a lawyer?   A: Yes.

What are they talking about?

WARMING UP

❏ Work with a partner.

What do you usually talk about when you meet someone for the first time?

What don't you talk about?

Check (✔) "yes" or "no" for each topic below and on page 37.

> This is a great party, isn't it?

the place you are at

☑ yes ☐ no

> What do you do?

jobs

☑ yes ☐ no

> How much money do you make?

salary

☐ yes ☑ no

> Would you like something to drink?

food and drink

☑ yes ☐ no

> Do you believe in God?

religion

☐ yes ☑ no

> Where are you from?

hometowns

☑ yes ☐ no

What are they talking about?

> ***Topic/function:*** Evaluating whether a topic
>   of conversation is appropriate
> ***Listening skills:*** Inferring topics (Listening
>   Task 1), understanding/inferring
>   relationships (Listening Task 2)
> ***Grammar/vocabulary:*** Question forms,
>   simple present

Warming Up

1. Hold your book so that students can see
pages 36 and 37. T: *Look at pages 36 and 37.*

2. Read the instructions:

> *Work with a partner.*
> *What do you usually talk about when you
>   meet someone for the first time?*
> *What don't you talk about?*
> *Check "yes" or "no" for each topic below and
>   on page 37.*

3. Demonstrate by doing the first two or
three as a full class. Ask this question: *When
you meet someone, do you talk about the place
you are at?* Have students raise their hands
to indicate "yes" or "no."

4. Have students work in pairs, checking
their answers for each. Make sure they
check answers on both pages 36 and 37. As
they work, circulate and help pairs having
difficulty. Check the understanding of
these pairs by asking questions as in step 3.

5. Don't check the answers yet. Students
will do that after completing Listening
Task 1.

NOTES

• This unit arose from problems foreign
students sometimes have with native
English speakers when the students use
conversational openers that are
appropriate in their cultures but
inappropriate in others.

Appropriateness varies with cultures,
and students are often not aware that they
are being rude when they bring up certain
topics.

The point of the unit is not to label
people "wrong." The point is to help
students survive in other cultures.

Strategy exercise: *Analyzing contrasting languages*

Teachers sometimes worry whether to let
students use what they know in their own
language(s). While we do not want to
encourage translation, there is a place for
contrasting languages. In this unit, it may
help to allow students to talk about or
share what is considered rude in their own
language(s). They can make lists of topics
or words they would use or not use with a
friend, their parents, a teacher, a stranger,
etc.

Optional activities

(For use anytime during or after the unit.)

• ***Meeting people.*** As a class, brainstorm
how to greet people and how to make
introductions. In pairs, students divide
these into formal and friendly and think of
situations where they might use each
expression.

• ***Talking to other people.*** In small groups,
have students brainstorm topics they
would talk about with their mother, with a
religious leader, a store clerk, and a person
on the bus.

Listening Task 1
I wouldn't ask that.

Note: The tapescript for Unit 11 begins on page T16.

1. T: *Look at page 37.*

2. (**Optional**) Read the title: *"I wouldn't ask that." What do you think this activity is about?* Elicit answers from the students. (Answer: topics of conversation that are inappropriate in English-speaking countries)

3. (**Optional**) If your students find listening very difficult, do the Additional Support procedure.

4. Read the instructions: *Listen. What are these people talking about? Circle the topics.*

5. Play Listening Task 1 on the tape. Gesture for students to circle the topics.

6. Stop the tape before the final instructions ("Look at the topics you circled . . . ").

7. (**Optional**) To make sure students understand what to do, stop after the first two segments. Ask students: *Which topics did they talk about?* Elicit answers (the places they are, jobs, etc.). Then play the rest of Listening Task 1.

8. If necessary, play Listening Task 1 a second time.

9. Check by eliciting answers from the students or by saying each topic and having students raise their hands if they circled it. (Answers appear in blue on the opposite page.)

10. Read the final instructions: *Look at the topics you circled. Did you check "yes" for these topics in Warming Up? Look at the topics you didn't circle. In English-speaking countries, people don't usually talk about these topics when they first meet.*

ADDITIONAL SUPPORT Additional support may not be necessary since the students will have worked with the topics in Warming Up. If you think they'll still have trouble, have them work in pairs. Have them read the sentences in the speech balloons. Tell them to imagine they are at a party. If a stranger said these sentences to them, how would they feel? They should cross out any that they don't like.

NOTES

• The context is a party in an English-speaking country. There are several people at the party who do not know each other. This situation is used to show how people talk to each other when they first meet. Generally, people try to find things they have in common, so they talk about the food and music at the party and about shared interests.

• The topics not mentioned on the tape are usually not discussed when people first meet. There are, of course, no absolute rules. Certain situations may allow these topics to be mentioned, but generally, they should be avoided.

Culture corner

1. After students have read the Culture Corner, have them work in small groups to compare answers to these questions: *How do you meet new people in your country? Do you introduce yourself?*

2. (**Optional**) After they have read the Culture Corner, have students work in groups of about three. Give them the following list of situations. For each, students think of an opening statement similar to the example.

  a. at a party   c. on a bus or train
  b. at school   d. at the beach

Answers might include things like:

  a. I like this music.
  b. This class is difficult, isn't it?
  c. Are you going to _____ *(place)* ?
  d. It's hot today, isn't it?

I wouldn't ask that.

❏ Listen. What are these people talking about?
Circle the topics.

❏ Look at the topics you circled.
Did you check "yes" for these topics in Warming Up?
Look at the topics you didn't circle.
In English-speaking countries, people don't usually talk about these topics
when they first meet.

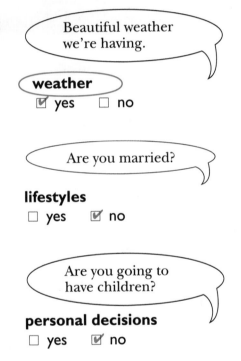

Beautiful weather
we're having.

weather
☑ yes   ☐ no

How old are you?

age
☐ yes   ☑ no

Are you married?

lifestyles
☐ yes   ☑ no

Do you like jazz?

likes and dislikes
☑ yes   ☐ no

Are you going to
have children?

personal decisions
☐ yes   ☑ no

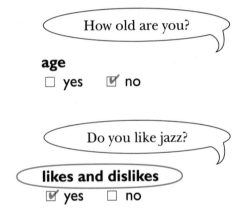

CULTURE CORNER

In English-speaking countries, it is usually OK to introduce yourself to other
people in class or at a party. You don't need to wait for someone to introduce
you. When people meet for the first time, they sometimes talk about the
situation before they introduce themselves. For example, they may find
something they agree on:

A: I think this will be an interesting class.
B: I think so too. By the way, I'm Jean.

How do you meet new people in your country? Do you introduce yourself?

LISTENING TASK 2.

A day in the life . . .

❏ Listen. Meg and Ted have a lot of different conversations during the day.
Who is Meg or Ted talking to? Match each conversation (1–6) with a picture.
Write the number in the box. There is one extra picture.
What helped you understand? Write at least one thing for each.

6

contract

meeting

_____

4

bowl is empty

get some water

go outside

2

get you changed

see Grandma

1

coffee

wife talking about plans for
the day

5

report

new system

proposal

3

late for school

homework/library books

help Grandma

YOUR TURN TO TALK

Work in groups of three. How many ways do you know to introduce yourself in
English? What else do you say when you meet someone for the first time?
Write your answers. Which are formal? Which are friendly?

Examples
I'm very pleased to meet you. (*formal*)
Hi. (*friendly*)

Listening Task 2
A day in the life . . .

> **Listening skill:** Understanding/inferring relationships

1. T: *Look at page 38.*

2. (**Optional**) Read the title: *"A day in the life . . ." What do you think this activity will be about?* Elicit answers from the students. (Answer: people the speakers talk to)

3. (**Optional**) If students find listening very difficult, do the Additional Support procedure.

4. Read the instructions: *Listen. Meg and Ted have a lot of different conversations during the day. Who is Meg or Ted talking to? Match each conversation with a picture. Write the number in the box. There is one extra picture. What helped you understand? Write at least one thing for each.*

5. Play Listening Task 2 on the tape. Gesture for students to number the pictures and write the words.

6. (**Optional**) To make sure students understand what to do, stop after the second conversation. Ask students: *Which picture?* (Answer: middle-left). *How did you know?* (get you changed, see Grandma, the speaker's tone of voice, etc.) Then play the rest of Listening Task 2.

7. If necessary, play Listening Task 2 a second time. Before replaying the tape, you may want to have students compare their answers in pairs. *Work with a partner. Look at your partner's answers. How many were the same? Then we'll listen again.*

8. Check by drawing squares on the board in the pattern of the pictures. Elicit answers from the students. (Answers appear in blue on the opposite page.) Most students will not have written all the "clues" provided.

ADDITIONAL SUPPORT Point out that sometimes we speak in a friendly, informal way. Other times, we are more formal and businesslike. Have students close their books. Write the following on the board:

Friendly					Formal
1	2	3	4	5	6

Have them listen and rate each conversation based on what they hear and the tone of voice. Exact answers will vary, but conversations 1 to 4 are friendly; conversations 5 and 6 are more formal.

NOTES

• This task follows a family through the day to illustrate the different ways people talk to family members and people at work. The father speaks to the baby about getting "changed." This refers to putting a new diaper on the baby. The mother speaks to her sons as "guys." This is a relatively common way to talk to a group of children or to friends, male or female (even though "a guy" is usually male).

Your turn to talk

1. Divide the class into groups of three. T: *Work in groups of three. How many ways do you know to introduce yourself in English? What else do you say when you meet someone for the first time? Write your answers. Which are formal? Which are friendly?*

2. (**Optional**) To help students get started, brainstorm ways to introduce oneself. Answers may include the following: I'm _____ . Hello. My name is _____. Can I introduce myself? It's nice to meet you. (I'm) pleased to meet you.

3. (after about 5 minutes) T: *What did you write?* As students call out answers, write them on the chalkboard. Have students decide whether the introductions are formal or friendly.

U N I T   1 2

How was your vacation?

Topic/function: Describing past activities
Listening skills: Understanding past
    activities, understanding emotions
    (Listening Task 1); following a story
    (Listening Task 2)
Grammar/vocabulary: Simple past tense

Warming Up

1. Hold your book so that students can see
page 39. T: *Look at page 39.*

2. Read the first part of the instructions.
> *What did you do on your last vacation?*
> *Check the things you did.*
> *Add something about each activity.*

3. Demonstrate by asking about one of the
items. T: *How many people visited relatives?*
When some students have raised their
hands, ask follow-up questions and gesture
for students to write that information: *Who
did you visit? Where do they live? Did you have
a good time?*

4. As students work, circulate and help
those having difficulty.

5. Read the second part of the
instructions:
> *Work with a partner.*
> *What activities did your partner check?*
> *Ask your partner about the vacation.*
> *Write three things your partner did.*

6. You may wish to follow up by reading
the items and having students raise their
hands to see how many did each thing.

NOTE

• In the unlikely event that some students
didn't do any of these things, have them
write at least three things they did do.
They could talk about a weekend or short
holiday they enjoyed.

Strategy exercise: Getting the idea quickly

Listening Task 1 presents two different
kinds of tasks. Students listen for what the
people did and whether they enjoyed
themselves. This might be a good time to
remind students that when they listen, they
listen for a purpose. In the first case, they
are listening for places and activities. In
the second, they are listening for
evaluations, words like "great," "boring,"
etc. Point out that they should use the
directions or the situation to help them
decide why they are listening. This will
focus their attention, and they will be able
to understand more quickly than they
could by worrying about all the
information they hear.

Optional activities

(For use anytime during or after the unit.)

• **Mouth marathon.** Have students working
in pairs describe their last vacation or what
would be an ideal vacation. They should
speak for as long as they can without
stopping. They can use fillers like "Uh,"
"What I mean to say is . . .," etc. They
cannot repeat information. Partners
should keep time. The person who talks
the longest wins the marathon.

• **Tell a "lie."** Have students work in pairs.
One tells the other something that
happened in the past. The speaker should
change three facts. The partner tries to
catch the "lies" in the story.

How was your vacation?

❑ What did you do on your last vacation?
   Check (✔) the things you did.
   Add something about each activity.

✔
☐ went hiking
☐ visited a museum
☐ visited relatives
☐ saw a movie
☐ went to a beach
☐ just rested
☐ went shopping
☐ read a book
☐ went camping
☐ visited a garden
☐ visited a famous place
☐ other

❑ Work with a partner.
   What activities did your partner check?
   Ask your partner about the vacation.
   Write three things your partner did.

SAMPLE
ANSWERS

Anna visited her grandparents.

She just rested and went shopping.

She read a book in English.

39

Did you have a good time?

❏ Listen. People are talking about their vacations.
Draw lines to the things they did.
Did they enjoy themselves? Complete the sentences.

I.

Kenji

Kenji's vacation was
great .

Laura's vacation was
nice and relaxing .

Laura   Laura   Kenji   Kenji   Laura

2.

Lisa

Lisa's vacation was
exciting .

Dave's vacation was
boring .

Dave   Lisa   Lisa   Lisa   Dave

CULTURE CORNER

Holidays are special days like New Year's when most people don't work. They include cultural, religious, and historical days. Vacation days are days that a person takes off from work. Work hours, holidays, and vacations differ a lot around the world. This chart shows averages for five countries.

Country	Work week	Holidays	Vacation
Britain and France	39 hours	8 days	25 days
Germany	38	10	30
Japan	42	20	16
The United States	40	10	12

How many hours a week do people work in your country? How much vacation do they have?

Listening Task 1
Did you have a good time?

Note: The tapescript for Unit 12 begins on
page T17.

1. T: *Look at page 40.*

2. (**Optional**) Read the title: *"Did you have
a good time?" What do you think this activity
will be about?* Elicit answers from the
students. (Answer: vacations)

3. (**Optional**) If students find listening
very difficult, do the Additional Support
procedure below.

4. Read the instructions: *Listen. People are
talking about their vacations. Draw lines to the
things they did. Did they enjoy themselves?
Complete the sentences.*

5. Play Listening Task 1 on the tape.
Gesture for students to write their answers.

6. (**Optional**) To make sure students
understand what to do, stop after two
items have been mentioned (Vancouver,
garden). Ask students: *Where did Kenji go?
What did he see there?* When students answer,
gesture for them to draw lines from Kenji
to the items. Then play the rest of
Listening Task 1.

7. If necessary, play Listening Task 1 a
second time.

8. Check by eliciting answers from the
students. (Answers appear in blue on the
opposite page. The words used to describe
the emotions may vary.)

ADDITIONAL SUPPORT Have students
work in pairs. Have them look at the
pictures. Tell them Kenji, Laura, Lisa, and
Dave each did at least two things. Have
them guess two things for each person. Of
course, they have no way of knowing, but
the process of guessing will make them
more familiar with the choices given and,

in many cases, will make their listening
more focused, since they want to find out
if they are correct.

NOTES

• The speakers use the simple past tense
because the actions they have done are
complete.

• The information in the Culture Corner
is from *Time* magazine (March 20, 1990).
According to *Time*, these are the number
of vacation days actually taken, not just
those allowed.

Culture corner

1. After they have read the Culture
Corner, ask a few students to answer the
following questions: *How many hours a week
do people work in your country? How much
vacation do they have?*

2. (**Optional**) Have students compare
their own schedules or those of their
family members with the information
given.

Listening Task 2
A weekend to remember
(unfortunately)

Listening skill: Following a story

1. T: *Look at page 41.*

2. (**Optional**) *Read the title: "A weekend to remember (unfortunately)." What do you think this activity will be about?* Elicit answers from the students. (Answer: a bad weekend/ camping trip)

3. (**Optional**) If students find listening very difficult, do the Additional Support procedure below.

4. Read the instructions: *Listen. Tom went camping last weekend. He didn't have a good time. Put the pictures in order.*

5. Play Listening Task 2 on the tape. Gesture for students to number the pictures.

6. (**Optional**) To make sure students understand what to do, stop after "You burned the steak?" Ask students: *Which picture is number two?* After they have answer, hold your book so that they can see it and gesture as if writing the number. Then play the rest of Listening Task 2.

7. If necessary, play Listening Task 2 a second time. You may want to encourage students who understood the order the first time to close their eyes and try to imagine the story.

8. Check by drawing eight boxes on the board to represent the pictures. Letter the boxes A–H. Have students call out the letters in order (number 1 is D, number 2 is E, etc.). (Answers appear in blue on the opposite page.)

ADDITIONAL SUPPORT Say one sentence describing what is happening in each picture (A man is sleeping in a car.) Students touch the picture described. If you are working with weakly motivated students, do this competitively. Have pairs of students put one book between them. Students race to touch the picture faster than their partners. The faster student gets one point.

NOTES

• Tom had a terrible time. He emphasizes this by using words like "a disaster," "to a crisp," and "poured," but he is talking about it in a humorous way. He sees how funny the series of bad luck is; people can have a little bad luck, but in his case everything went wrong.

Your turn to talk

Note: This activity often works best when students stand in circles.

1. Divide the class into groups. T: *Work in groups of five. You are going to tell a chain story. It should be an adventure story. One person begins. Start like this: Once upon a time, (*name*) went to (*place*). Someone else says the next sentence. Each person adds a new sentence to the story. Use some of these words.* Point to the words in the box.

2. Demonstrate how the story works by beginning the story; encourage a few students to continue it. T: *Once upon a time, Tom Cruise went to Thailand.*

3. Have the students begin. They can either continue their story in the circle or people can offer the next sentences anytime without waiting for a turn.

LISTENING TASK 2

A weekend to remember (unfortunately)

❏ Listen. Tom went camping last weekend.
He didn't have a good time.
Put the pictures in order (1–8).

 4

 6

 8

 1

 2

 7

 5

 3

YOUR TURN TO TALK

Work in groups of five. You are going to tell a chain story. It should be an adventure story. One person begins. That person says the first sentence. Start like this:

Once upon a time ___(name)___ went to ___(place)___.

Someone else says the next sentence. Each person adds a new sentence to the story. Use some of these words:

skiing	crocodile	helicopter	president or prime minister
ice cream	beautiful	bomb	flamingo
expensive	birthday	gold	

Around the house

What jobs do you enjoy doing at home?
Which do you dislike doing?

❏ Look at these household tasks.
Which do you dislike? Cross (**X**) them out.
Are there any you like? Circle them.

	cleaning		cooking
	doing laundry		vacuuming
	washing dishes		washing windows

❏ Write at least three more household tasks.
Do you like to do them or not?

SAMPLE
ANSWERS

   ironing

   mopping the floor

   dusting

❏ Work with a partner.
How many of your answers were the same?
Which tasks do you like the most?
Which do you hate?

U N I T 1 3
Around the house

> ***Topic/function:*** Talking about household
>   jobs and chores
> ***Listening skills:*** Identifying attitudes
>   (Listening Task 1), identifying
>   preferences (Listening Task 2)
> ***Grammar/vocabulary:*** Gerunds (-*ing*
>   forms), infinitives

Warming Up

1. (**Optional**) Begin by brainstorming household tasks (cleaning, washing dishes, etc.). List as many as possible on the board. Students include them with those in the book when they are identifying the ones they like and dislike.

2. Hold your book so that students can see page 42. T: *Look at page 42.*

3. Read the first set of instructions. Pause when you see the symbol ♦ to give students time to answer the questions.

> *What jobs do you enjoy doing at home?*
> *Which do you dislike doing?*
> *Look at these household tasks.*
> *Which do you dislike? Cross them out. Are
>   there any you like? Circle them.* ♦
> *Write at least three more household tasks. Do
>   you like to do them or not?* ♦

4. Demonstrate by asking several students: *Which do you dislike? Are there any you like?* Gesture for them to write Xs and draw circles to indicate their opinions.

5. As students work, circulate and help those having difficulty.

6. Read the instructions for the last part.
> *Work with a partner.*
> *How many of your answers were the same?*
> *Which tasks do you like the most?*
> *Which do you hate?*

7. You may want to poll the class at the end to see which task is the most disliked.

Do this by having each student decide on the single most hated task. Call out the choices and have students raise their hands if it is their least favorite.

NOTES

• Although some people have not worked extensively around the house, everyone has probably washed dishes or cleaned a room. Encourage students to use whatever experience they have, or their imagination.

Strategy exercise: Making positive statements

By now, students are more than half way through the book. They may feel restless with the school term and in need of encouragement. Now might be a good time to review the goals you talked about in the beginning of the term and see how much progress has been made. Students should think of one positive thing they have accomplished, or one activity they really enjoyed doing or did well. They may prefer not to say which it is. It is adequate to have them think about or write down something they are happy with. Stress the positive, and stress the importance of positive thinking (not getting discouraged) in language learning.

Optional activities

(For use anytime during or after the unit.)

• ***Same or different?*** Have students working in pairs make a list of the things they agree on–the things they both like to do at work or at school.

• ***Good excuse.*** Have students working in pairs look at Listening Task 1. Ask them to write down good excuses for not doing those things. Then have pairs work with two other pairs and combine lists. They should cross out any excuses that more than one group has written. The group with the most original excuses wins.

Listening Task 1
I hate doing that.

Note: The tapescript for Unit 13 begins on p. T18.

1. T: *Look at page 43.*

2. (**Optional**) Read the title: *"I hate doing that!" What do you think this activity will be about?* Elicit answers from the students. (Answer: how people feel about things/tasks people hate)

3. (**Optional**) If students find listening very difficult, do the Additional Support procedure below.

4. Read the instructions: *Listen. People are talking about jobs around the house and other chores. Do they like them or dislike them? Draw lines to show how strongly they feel.*

5. Play Listening Task 1 on the tape. Gesture for students to draw lines.

6. (**Optional**) To make sure students understand what to do, stop after the second item. Draw the smiling and frowning faces on the board. Ask students: *Where did you draw the line? Should I go left or right? Tell me when to stop.* Move your hand until they tell you to stop. Then play the rest of Listening Task 1.

7. If necessary, play Listening Task 1 a second time.

8. Check by drawing the faces on the board (see step 6). Elicit responses. (Approximate answers appear in blue on opposite page.)

ADDITIONAL SUPPORT Write the following words on the board: *co-workers, friends, husband/wife.* Play the tape one time. Have students guess the relationship of the speakers. The answers are as follows: (1) friends, (2) husband/wife,

(3) co-workers, (4) roommates, (5) roommates, (6) co-workers.

NOTES

• Some students may initially be uncomfortable that there is no exact "right or wrong" position on the line. Point out that feelings are not exact. The speaker's tone of voice and the speaker's vocabulary give clues about how strong the feeling is.

• Some verbs link with other verbs using either the gerund (verb + -ing form: "I hate cleaning my office") or the infinitive (verb + to form: "I hate to clean my office"). Others take only one form or the other ("I enjoy giving the baby a bath," but not "I enjoy to give. . . "; "I want to do laundry," but not "I want doing laundry"). The difference is that the -ing form sounds slightly more real and immediate than the infinitive form. However, this "rule" is probably too vague and abstract to be of practical use to most students.

Culture corner

1. After they have read the Culture Corner, ask a few students to answer the question: *What jobs around the house do you think are the most unpopular in your country?*

2. (**Optional**) After reading the Culture Corner, have each student write six sentences comparing bits of information. Two or three of the sentences should be false. The others are true. Each sentence must contain one of these words: *more, less, fewer, like, dislike, hate.* For example: "More people hate ironing than doing laundry." Then have students work in groups of three or four. They read their sentences. Partners race to say whether they are true or false.

I hate doing that!

❏ Listen. People are talking about jobs around the house and other chores.
Do they like them or dislike them?
Draw lines to show how strongly they feel.

likes	so-so	dislikes
😊	😐	😠

1. cooking

2. washing floors

3. giving the baby a bath

4. doing laundry

5. washing dishes

6. cleaning the office

CULTURE CORNER

These are the 10 most unpopular household tasks in the United States and Canada. The percentage shows the number of people who dislike this task more than any other.

1. washing dishes	17.0%	6. vacuuming	6.2%
2. cleaning the bathroom	8.8	7. washing windows	4.9
3. ironing	8.5	8. cooking	4.8
4. washing floors	7.5	9. doing laundry	4.7
5. cleaning	7.3	10. dusting	4.7

What jobs around the house do you think are the most unpopular in your country?

I agree!

❏ Listen. Does the man like these things?
Check (✔) "likes" or "dislikes."
Why? Write his reasons.

❏ Do you agree? Circle "I agree" or "I don't agree."

Your opinion

1. Working at home
    ☑ likes
    ❏ dislikes
    Why? _quieter, doesn't have to drive_

I agree.
I don't agree.

2. Cooking
    ☑ likes
    ❏ dislikes
    Why? _relaxing_

I agree.
I don't agree.

3. Reading nonfiction
    ☑ likes
    ❏ dislikes
    Why? _learns a lot_

I agree.
I don't agree.

4. Growing flowers
    ❏ likes
    ☑ dislikes
    Why? _too much work_

I agree.
I don't agree.

5. Driving
    ❏ likes
    ☑ dislikes
    Why? _hates traffic_

I agree.
I don't agree.

YOUR TURN TO TALK

Imagine your "dream house." What would it have? A swimming pool? A marble fireplace? A big yard? A tennis court? Think for one minute. Then work in groups of three. Describe your dream houses. What features do you all want? What do your partners want that you don't?

Listening Task 2 I agree!

I. T: *Look at page 44.*

2. (**Optional**) Read the title: *"I agree!"*
What do you think this activity will be about?
Elicit answers from the students. (Answer:
opinions about the items illustrated)

3. (**Optional**) If students find listening
very difficult, do the Additional Support
procedure.

4. Read the first part of the instructions:
*Listen. Does the man like these things? Check
"likes" or "dislikes." Why? Write his reasons.*

5. Play the first segment of Listening Task
2 on the tape. Gesture for students to write
their answers.

6. If necessary, play Listening Task 2 a
second time. Before replaying the tape,
you may want to have students compare
their answers in pairs: *Work with a partner.
Look at what your partner wrote about the man.
How many answers were the same? Then we'll
listen again.*

7. Check by saying the topics. Have
students raise their hands to show if the
man likes or dislikes the items. Elicit their
answers to the reasons. (Answers appear in
blue on the opposite page.)

8. Read the second part of the
instructions: *Do your agree? Circle "I agree" or
"I don't agree."* Make sure students
understand that the "I agree/ I don't
agree" section is their own opinion, not
something on the tape. Gesture for them
to circle their opinions.

9. Have students raise their hands to
indicate their own opinions.

  Variation: Instead of having students
give their opinions after completing the
activity, have them circle "I agree" or "I
disagree" as they listen.

ADDITIONAL SUPPORT Have students look
at the items illustrated. To the right of the
"I agree/I don't agree" sentences, they
mark whether or not they like these things.
This can be done by writing "yes" and "no"
or by drawing smiling and frowning faces.

NOTES

• Make sure that students are comparing
their opinions to the man's. When
students disagree with the man's negative
opinions (growing flowers and driving), it
means they like these things.

• One way to talk about what you like to
do is to say you're "into it." "It's a pain" is
an informal way to say you don't like
something.

• The man is talking about working at
home instead of going to an office.

Your turn to talk

I. (**Optional**) Have students close their
eyes and imagine their dream house as you
give the instructions to this activity. Speak
slowly and allow them time to get a mental
picture of the house.

2. T: *Imagine your "dream house." What
would it have? A swimming pool? A marble
fireplace? A big yard? A tennis court? Think for
one minute.* Allow time for students to
think.

3. Divide the class into groups of three. T:
*Work in groups of three. Describe your dream
houses. What features do you all want? What do
your partners want that you don't?*

4. As they work, circulate and help with
vocabulary.

U N I T   1 4
Shopping

> **Topic/funtion:** Talking about shopping for
> clothes and household items
> **Listening skills:** Understanding
> descriptions (Listening Task 1),
> inferring decisions (Listening Task 2)
> **Grammar/vocabulary:** Existential *to be*,
> descriptive adjectives (things)

Warming Up

1. Hold your book so that students can see
page 45. T: *Look at page 45.*

2. Read the instructions:

> *This is a shopping survey.*
> *It asks about your shopping habits.*
> *Work with a partner.*
> *First write your answers.*
> *Then ask your partner the questions.*
> *Write your partner's answers.*

3. Demonstrate by directing one pair
through the first step of the activity as
other students watch. T: (to Student A) *Do
you enjoy shopping? Write your answer. Now
ask your partner.* Point to question one in
A's book to cue that student to ask.

4. As students work, circulate and help
pairs having difficulty.

5. You may wish to follow up by asking the
questions to the entire class.

NOTES

• Both listening tasks in this unit help
students practice inference. If you think
your class will have trouble with this skill,
you might play a game to get them in the
mood to guess. For example, think of an
object in the classroom. Give two or three
hints about it and encourage students to
guess the object. Example: a chair. *I'm
looking for one to go with the desk. It's got to be
comfortable. Brown or black would be nice.*

Strategy exercise: *Seeing their own
progress*

Sometimes it is difficult for students at this
level to see their own progress. When they
were beginners, everything they learned
was clearly new. Now, although they are
moving ahead, they may not see it because
the steps they take are smaller in relation
to all the English they already know. To
help students see their progress, choose a
listening task they found challenging
earlier in the course . Before they listen,
have them work in pairs, listing whatever
they remember about doing the activity
(the speed, difficult vocabulary, etc.).
Then play the tape. Most students will be
surprised to see how much easier it is.

Optional activities

(For use anytime during or after the unit.)

• ***We're going shopping.*** Work as a whole
class or in groups of six to eight. The first
student says, "We're going shopping and
we're going to buy (something beginning
with "a"). The second person repeats this
and adds something beginning with "b."
The third person repeats both and adds a
"c" word. With the whole class, you might
want to call on students out of turn so that
all will have to listen. You might want to
eliminate the letter "x." Students should
not take notes; the fun is in trying to
remember.

• ***Don't say "no."*** Students work in pairs.
One student is a salesperson, the other is a
customer. The salesperson wants to sell the
customer a huge TV and tells the customer
why he or she should buy it. The customer
does not want to buy it. The customer
answers the salesperson, but cannot say
"no." The customer must give a reason
each time. For example:

Salesperson: This is the newest TV in the
  store.

Customer: I like old things.

Shopping

This is a shopping survey.
It asks about your shopping habits.

❑ Work with a partner.
First write your answers.
Then ask your partner the questions.
Write your partner's answers.

Shopping Survey

	You	*Your partner*
1. Do you enjoy shopping?	_____	_____
2. How often do you go shopping?	_____ (times a week/month)	_____
3. What do you like to shop for?	_____	_____
4. Do you like to shop alone or with someone?	_____	_____
5. Have you ever shopped by mail or telephone?	_____	_____

It's perfect!

❏ Listen. Some people are shopping. What are they buying?
Match each conversation (1–5) with a picture.
Write the number in the box. There are three extra pictures.

5

1

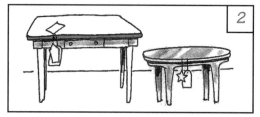
3

2

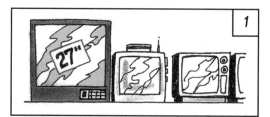
4

CULTURE CORNER

Most cultures have sayings about money. In the English-speaking world, people say "A penny saved is a penny earned." A penny is one cent. It isn't worth very much, but the proverb says even small amounts are valuable. The Japanese have a similar saying: "If you laugh at one yen, you will cry for one yen." A saying from Britain warns about being too worried about spending money. It is "Penny wise but pound foolish." It means that if you always buy the cheapest thing or try not to spend a penny, you will end up spending a pound – 100 times as much. Money is important in most cultures. How important? In India there is this saying: "If you say 'money,' even the dead will come alive." Are there sayings about money in your language?

Listening Task I It's perfect!

Listening skill: Understanding descriptions

Note: The tapescript for Unit 14 begins on page T19.

I. T: *Look at page 46.*

2. (Optional) Read the title: *"It's perfect!" What do you think this activity will be about?* Elicit answers from the students. (Answer: people deciding on things to buy)

3. (Optional) If students find listening very difficult, do the Additional Support procedure below.

4. Read the instructions: *Listen. Some people are shopping. What are they buying? Match each conversation with a picture. Write the number in the box. There are three extra pictures.*

5. Play Listening Task 1 on the tape. Gesture for students to write their answers.

6. (Optional) To make sure students understand what to do, stop after the second conversation. Ask students: *What is she shopping for?* (Answer: the table) Then play the rest of Listening Task 1.

7. If necessary, play Listening Task 1 a second time.

8. Check by eliciting answers from the students. (Answers appear in blue on the opposite page.)

ADDITIONAL SUPPORT Have students work in pairs. Ask them to think of at least two adjectives describing each picture. To make sure they use a lot of different adjectives, they can use each only one time. Then have them write the adjectives next to the pictures. To give a gamelike feeling to the exercise, have them look at the pictures for about 30 seconds. Then they close their books and try to remember all the pictures, adding the adjectives to their descriptions.

Culture Corner

I. After students have read the Culture Corner, have them compare answers to this question: *Are there sayings about money in your language?*

2. (Optional) Students become better readers if they read in phrases (units of meaning) instead of word by word. After they read this Culture Corner, read the first two sentences to them. Pause slightly when you see the symbol //. Ask students to listen and mark the pauses by drawing lines where they hear each pause. Then have students work in pairs. Give one student a copy of A (below), and the other a copy of B (below). One student reads the sentences, pausing as indicated. Partners mark the pauses in their books, then read the paragraph back to check.

Most cultures // have sayings // about money. // In the English-speaking world, // people say // "A penny saved // is a penny earned."

A

A penny // is one cent. // It isn't worth very much, // but the proverb says // even small amounts // are valuable. // The Japanese // have a similar saying: // "If you laugh at one yen, // you will cry for one yen." // A saying from Britain // warns about being too worried // about spending money. // It is // "Penny wise // but pound foolish."

B

It means // that if you // always buy the cheapest thing // or try not to spend a penny, // they will end up spending a pound //100 times as much. // Money is important // in most cultures. // How important? // In India // there is this saying: // If you say 'money,' // even the dead // will come alive." // Are there sayings // about money // in your language?

Listening Task 2 I'll take it.

Listening skill: Inferring decisions

1. T: *Look at page 47.*

2. (**Optional**) Read the title: *"I'll take it."* *What do you think this activity will be about?* Elicit answers from the students. (Answer: decisions to buy things)

3. (**Optional**) If students find listening very difficult, do the Additional Support procedure below.

4. Read the instructions: *Listen. People are shopping. Do you think they will buy these things? Circle "yes" or "no." When the answer is "no," write the reason.*

5. Play Listening Task 2 on the tape. Gesture for students to circle their answers and write reasons.

6. (**Optional**) To make sure students understand what to do, stop after number three. Elicit answers from the students. Then play the rest of Listening Task 2.

7. If necessary, play Listening Task 2 a second time. Before replaying the tape, you may want to have students compare their answers in pairs. *Work with a partner. Look at your partner's answers. How many were the same? Then we'll listen again.*

8. Check by eliciting answers from the students. (Answers appear in blue on the opposite page.)

ADDITIONAL SUPPORT Have students work in groups of about four. Ask them to look at all the pictures. For each one, think of at least two reasons not to buy the item. For example, for the CD player, they might not buy it because it's too expensive, of poor quality, a brand they don't know or trust, etc.

NOTES

• Tasks in this unit feature U.S. shopping routines. It is customary for the sales clerk to be relatively aggressive with customers, asking them if they need help or waiting nearby as they look at the items they want.

• You may prefer to check after each segment rather than waiting until students have heard all six parts.

Your turn to talk

1. Divide the class into groups of three. T: *Work in groups of three. Imagine that you are buying gifts. Think of one gift for each category below. What would you buy? Where would you buy it? Who would you give it to?*

2. Do item one as an example. T: *You are giving an expensive gift. What is the gift?* Elicit suggestions.

3. (**Optional**) (after about five minutes) T: *What was your most interesting or unusual gift? Each group choose one. Tell the class.*

LISTENING TASK 2

I'll take it.

❑ Listen. People are shopping.
Do you think they will buy these things?
Circle "yes" or "no." When the answer is "no," write the reason.

1. the jacket

yes   (no)

He doesn't like the design.

2. the CD player

(yes)   no

_____

3. the cordless phone

yes   (no)

They don't know the brand.

4. the jeans

yes   (no)

They are the wrong size.

5. the computer

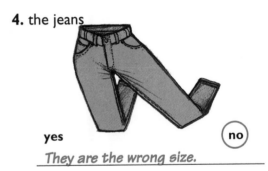

(yes)   no

_____

6. the notebook

yes   (no)

It doesn't have enough pages.

YOUR TURN TO TALK

Work in groups of three. Imagine that you are buying gifts. Think of one gift for each category below. What would you buy? Where would you buy it? Who would you give it to?

something expensive   something very cheap
something funny or crazy   something practical and useful
something romantic   something for your teacher

Going places

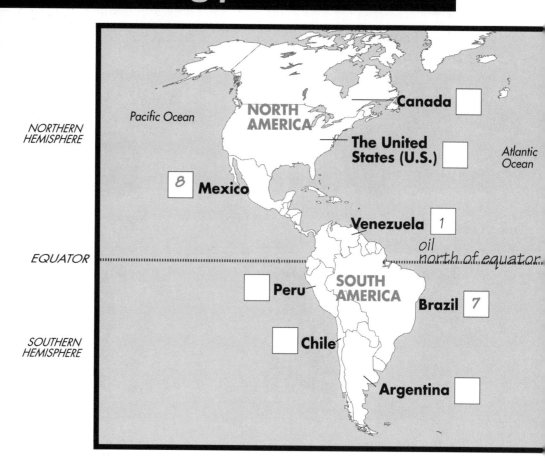

NORTHERN
HEMISPHERE

Pacific Ocean

NORTH
AMERICA

Canada ☐

The United
States (U.S.) ☐

Atlantic
Ocean

⟨8⟩ Mexico

Venezuela ⟨1⟩

oil
north of equator

EQUATOR

SOUTH
AMERICA

☐ Peru

Brazil ⟨7⟩

SOUTHERN
HEMISPHERE

☐ Chile

Argentina ☐

WARMING
UP

❑ Work with a partner.
   Answer these questions. Listen to your partner's answers.
   (Other countries are labeled on pages 66 and 67.)

1. If you could go to any country in the world, where would you go?
2. What country would you not want to visit? Why?
3. Which place in your country is the most interesting for tourists
   from other countries?
4. What things about your country are hard for foreigners to
   understand?

U N I T   1 5
Going places

Topic/ function: Talking about and
  comparing countries
Listening skills: Identifying places
  (Listening Task 1), understanding
  questions and answers (Listening Task 2)
Grammar/vocabulary: Comparatives

Warming Up

1. Hold your book so that students can see
page 48. T: *Look at pages 48 and 49.*

2. Read the instructions:

Work with a partner.
Answer these questions.
Listen to your partner's answers.

3. As students work, circulate and help
pairs having difficulty. Check
understanding by asking the questions on
the page.

4. (**Optional**) As some pairs finish, you
may want them to form groups of four to
compare answers.

5. (**Optional**) Compare answers as a full
class. Have individuals say their answers.
Students with the same answers raise their
hands.

NOTES

• Encourage students to be creative and
to think about *anywhere*, not just the most
popular places. If you have students from
many countries, you might want to handle
the question "What country would you not
want to visit?" carefully.

• The map helps focus the students on
possible answers. It cannot name all
countries. A more completely labeled map
can be found on pages 66 and 67.

Strategy exercise: *Reviewing*

Students can profit by learning how others
review. A useful review technique is
"spiraling." Spiraling means reviewing
material on the day you learn it, then the
next day, then two days later, then at ever-
increasing intervals (but always reviewing).
The key is putting the information into a
variety of contexts (new sentences,
associations, etc.). Different systems of
review work for different kinds of learners.
Encourage students to learn new ways
from their peers and to try at least one
new way this week.

Optional activity

(For use anytime during or after the unit.)

• Have students, working in groups of
four or five, continue playing the game
introduced in Listening Task 1. Using
either the map on these pages or the one
on pages 66 and 67, they take turns
thinking of countries and giving hints. The
hints are based on information they know.
If possible, students should start with
general hints and move toward more
specific information.

Listening Task 1
How much do you know?

Listening skill: Identifying places

Note: The tapescript for Unit 15 begins on page T21.

1. T: *Look at pages 48 and 49.*

2. (**Optional**) Read the title: *"How much do you know?" What do you think this will be about?* Elicit answers from the students. (Answer: information about countries)

3. (**Optional**) If students find listening very difficult, do the Additional Support procedure below.

4. Read the instructions: *Listen. You are going to take a "quiz" on countries. Look at the map. Which countries is the speaker talking about? Write the numbers in the boxes. What information helped you guess each country? Write your answers.*

5. Play Listening Task 1 on the tape. Gesture for students to write their answers.

6. (**Optional**) To make sure students understand what to do, stop after item two. Ask students: *What country is number 2?* (answer: India) *How did you know?* (Likely answers: Northern Hemisphere, old culture, in Asia, southwest of China, many languages) Then play the rest of Listening Task 1.

7. If necessary, play Listening Task 1 a second time.

8. Check by having students call out the answers and the words that helped them understand. (Answers appear in blue on pages 48 and 49.)

ADDITIONAL SUPPORT Have students, working in pairs or small groups, look at the countries labeled on the map and try to say one thing about each. Information could include location, capitals or large cities, languages, or products the countries are known for.

- You might want to review or preteach geography terms like *equator* and *hemisphere*, but do not give away too much information. To be safe, use countries you are sure students will know.

- Students may be surprised to hear that India has over 800 languages. The most common are Hindi, English, and Bengali. If dialects are counted, the country has about 1,650 languages.

Culture corner

1. After students have read the Culture Corner, ask a few to answer the questions: *What is your country's largest city? Why have people come to live there?*

2. (**Optional**) Before students read the Culture Corner, have them close their books. Dictate the names of the following cities as students write them: *Mexico City, São Paulo, Seoul, Tokyo.* Tell students you are going to say the populations of the cities in the wrong order. They should listen and write each population next to the city they think has that population. Dictate the numbers in this order:

> *15 million*
>
> *27 million*
>
> *18 million*
>
> *16 million*

After the students have written their guesses, have them read to find out whether or not their guesses were correct.

Note: It is difficult to estimate populations of huge cities because various countries use different counting procedures. The estimates here are based on the greater metropolitan area of each city. They were reported by UPI-Kyodo Dec. 8, 1991.

2. India
Northern Hemisphere southwest of China
English, Hindi, and Bengali

3. Indonesia
Asia
many islands
Jakarta

4. Italy
on Mediterranean Sea
southern Europe
shaped like a boot

5. Egypt
Nile River
northeastern Africa

6. The Philippines
island country
many languages (including Tagalog)
Manila

7. Brazil
São Paulo and Rio
beautiful beaches
largest population in South America

8. Mexico
Northern Hemisphere
oil
largest city in North America

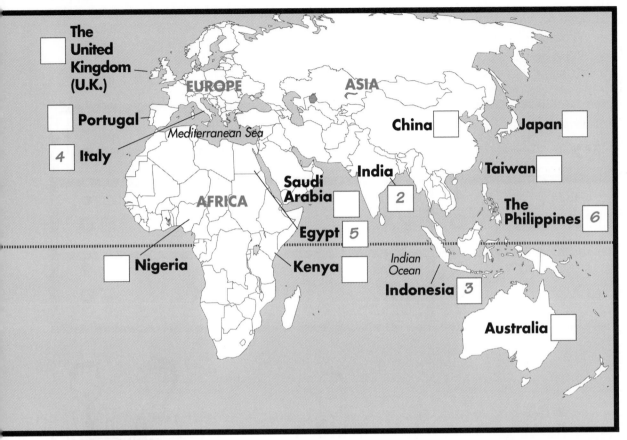

Identifying places

How much do you know?

❑ Listen. You are going to take a "quiz" on countries.
Look at the map. Which countries is the speaker talking about?
Write the numbers in the boxes.
What information helped you guess each country? Write your answers.

CULTURE CORNER

In the year 1578, Beijing was the world's largest city. It had 707,000 people. In the 1800s, London was the largest. It grew from 1,117,290 in 1801 to a peak of 8,615,050 in 1939. In 1957, Tokyo had the most people: 8,415,400. Now the world's four largest urban areas are Tokyo (27 million), São Paulo (18 million), Seoul (16 million), and Mexico City (15 million). What is your country's largest city? Why have people come to live there?

LISTENING TASK 2

Game show

❏ Listen. Two people are playing a TV game show.
What are the correct answers? Write each country or place.
Who gets the points? Check **X** for the woman's points.
Check **O** for the man's points.

Europe **1**	Cairo **2**	France **3**
☑**X** ☐**O**	☑**X** ☐**O**	☐**X** ☑**O**

Sweden **4**	Thailand **5**	Tokyo **6**
☐**X** ☑**O**	☑**X** ☐**O**	☑**X** ☐**O**

7	Hawaii **8**	Brazil **9**
☐**X** ☐**O**	☑**X** ☐**O**	☐**X** ☑**O**

Work with a partner. This is a speaking contest. See how long you can speak.
Your turn is over when you say something that is not in English or you stop for five seconds. Choose a topic:
   • The place I would most like to visit.
   • The best place for tourists in my country.
Your partner will listen and keep time. Then your partner speaks. When you finish, find a new partner and begin again.

Listening Task 2 Game show

1. T: *Look at page 50.*

2. (**Optional**) Read the title: *"Game show." What do you think this activity will be about?* Elicit answers from the students. (Answer: a TV quiz show based on information about various countries)

3. (**Optional**) If students find listening very difficult, do the Additional Support procedure below.

4. Read the instructions: *Listen. Two people are playing a TV game show. What are the correct answers? Write each country or place. Who gets the points? Check "X" for the woman's points. Check "O" for the man's points.*

5. Play Listening Task 2 on the tape. Gesture for students to write the answers and check "X" or "O."

6. (**Optional**) To make sure students understand what to do, stop after the first two questions. Have students say the answers. Then play the rest of Listening Task 2.

7. If necessary, play Listening Task 2 a second time. Before replaying the tape, you may want to have students compare their answers in pairs. *Work with a partner. Look at your partner's answers. How many were the same? Then we'll listen again.*

8. Check by having students call out their answers. You may wish to make a grid on the board to write the answers as they say them. (Answers appear in blue on the opposite page.)

ADDITIONAL SUPPORT Have students, working in pairs, look at the map on pages 66 and 67. Play the tape once. Students listen only for the names of the countries mentioned. They touch each country as soon as they hear it. Doing this in pairs encourages students to help each other and to compete to find the country first. This competition increases interest.

NOTES

• You might want to stop the tape and let students play along with the game. Students guess the answers before the correct answer is stated on the tape.

• Adjectives with one syllable and those with two syllables ending in "y" take "-er" and "-est": old, older, oldest and happy, happier, happiest. Most two-syllable adjectives that do not end in "y" and adjectives with three or more syllables take "more" and "most": beautiful, more beautiful, most beautiful.

Your turn to talk

1. Divide the class into pairs. T: *Work with a partner. This is a speaking contest. See how long you can speak. Your turn is over when you say something that is not in English or when you stop for five seconds.*

2. T: *Choose a topic: The place I would most like to visit. The best place for tourists in my country.* You may want to give students a minute or two to think about what they will say.

3. T: *Your partner will listen and keep time. Then your partner speaks. When you finish, find a new partner and begin again.*

Note: It is unusual for a student to speak longer than about three minutes without pausing for five seconds. It is useful to have partners time pauses by counting on their fingers behind their backs. This way, if the speaker has stopped, he or she won't see the partner counting, which increases nervousness and makes it hard to start again.

UNIT 16
Making plans

Topics/functions: Making and changing plans
Listening skills: Identifying times and places (Listening Task 1), identifying times (Listening Task 2)
Grammar/vocabulary: Future with *will*, future with *going to*

Warming Up

I. Hold your book so that students can see page 51. T: *Look at page 51.*

2. Read the instructions: *Will you do any of these things this month? Check the ones you'll do. When? Write your answers.*

3. T: *Work with a partner. Which things will your partner do? When?*

4. As students work, circulate and help pairs having difficulty. Check students' understanding by asking any of the questions from the chart.

5. (As some pairs finish) T: *Which of your partner's answers were the most interesting? Ask at least two more questions about them.*

6. Compare to see which activities most people will do by calling out each item and having students raise their hands if they are planning to do it.

NOTES

• In the unlikely event that a pair says they won't do any of the things, have them write things they will do and ask each other.

• The three most common ways of talking about the future in English are *will*, *going to* and the present progressive (*be* verb + *-ing*). Although usage is complex, in general, *will* is used to predict what will happen. "She will be a very good teacher." It is also used when the speaker is making a quick decision. "The phone's ringing. I'll

get it." *Going to* is used when plans have been made. "We're going to the baseball game on Saturday. Sue's going to drive." The present progressive is also used when decisions are certain. "I'm meeting her tomorrow."

Strategy exercise: *Language learning diary*

In keeping with the theme of the unit, students can be introduced to the idea of keeping a language learning diary. Some people list words they learn, others note questions they want to ask the teacher. Pairs might work on the design of a diary. T: *What is important for you to note and why? When will you use the diary?*

Optional activities

(For use anytime during or after the unit.)

• *Area tour.* Have students, working in groups of three, plan a one-day tour of their city or area for a foreign visitor. They should think of an identity for the visitor (student? businessperson? someone interested in sports? someone who likes cultural activities?) before they begin planning.

• *Class poll.* Write the following on the board.

1. your favorite quiet place
2. your favorite place to watch or play sports
3. your favorite entertainment place
4. your favorite restaurant (place for a good meal)
5. your favorite fast-food restaurant
6. your favorite view

Have each student write answers for the above. Then have them ask five other students if they agree (Is . . . your favorite . . . ?). They should add up the number of "yes" answers they get. The person with the fewest "yes" answers has the most unique preferences.

Making plans

❑ Will you do any of these things this month?
Check (✔) the ones you'll do.
When? Write your answers.

❑ Work with a partner.
Which things will your partner do? When?

	You	When	Your partner	When
Go to a party				
Take a trip				
Do something you don't want to do				
See a movie or video				
Watch or play sports				
Go to a restaurant with a friend				
Do something that will make you tired				
Go to a concert				

❑ Which of your partner's answers were the most interesting?
Ask at least two more questions about them.

Can we change the time?

❑ Listen. Some people have a change in plans.
Cross out the old information.
Write the new information.

1.

MONDAY 21	THURSDAY 24
TUESDAY 22 Lunch with Tony 12:00 ~~Bangkok~~ Cafe PLAZA	FRIDAY 25
WEDNESDAY 23	SATURDAY 26
	27 SUNDAY

2.

THURSDAY _____

FRIDAY _____

Concert 7:30 Hayes Hall
~~Meet in front~~
at 6:00 at Museum Cafe

SATURDAY _____

3.

Departures

Flight	Destination	Time	Gate
UA528	Tokyo	4:16	6
NA475	Seattle	6:00 ~~4:25~~	12
NW723	Toronto	4:40	7
CN305	São Paulo	4:50	5
CA39	Taipei	5:10	11

4.

SUN	MON	TUE	WED	THU	FRI	SAT
			1	2	3	4
5	6	7	8	9	10	11
12	13	14	15	16	17	18
			22	23	24	25

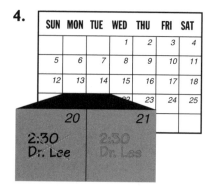

20	21
2:30 Dr. Lee	~~2:30~~ ~~Dr. Lee~~

CULTURE CORNER

Customs about time differ greatly around the world. In the United States and Canada, you should be on time for a business meeting, but a little (10 or 15 minutes) late if you are invited to a party at someone's house. Never arrive at a party early. But when meeting friends somewhere, in a restaurant for example, try to arrive on time. What are some of the time customs in your country?

Listening Task 1
Can we change the time?

Listening skills: Identifying times and places

Note: The tapescript for Unit 16 begins on page T22.

1. T: *Look at page 52.*

2. (**Optional**) Read the title: *"Can we change the time?" What do you think this activity will be about?* Elicit answers from the students. (Answer: changing plans)

3. (**Optional**) If students find listening very difficult, do the Additional Support procedure below.

4. Read the instructions: *Listen. Some people have a change in plans. Cross out the old information. Write the new information.*

5. Play Listening Task 1 on the tape. Gesture for students to write the changes.

6. (**Optional**) To make sure students understand what to do, stop after the second item. Ask students what answers they wrote.

7. If necessary, play Listening Task 1 a second time.

8. Check by having students call out the answers. As they do, write the correct information on the board. (Answers appear in blue on the opposite page.)

ADDITIONAL SUPPORT To give students more practice understanding times, have them work in pairs. Write "What time do you _____?" on the board. Students ask each other about their daily schedules. In a set time period of about five minutes they see how many things they do (other than this class) at the same time.

NOTES

• Listening Task 1 is centered on changing plans. In general, changing plans is not a problem in North American culture if enough advance notice is given. The apologies that are made are usually very quick and matter-of-fact.

Culture corner

1. After students have read the Culture Corner, have them compare answers to this question: *What are some of the time customs in your country?*

2. (**Optional**) Before students read the Culture Corner, write the following on the board:

a business meeting
a party at someone's house
meeting friends in a restaurant

In pairs, have students decide whether, in their culture(s), one should be early, on time, or a little late. Then have them read the Culture Corner to find out whether the cultural "rules" are the same in the United States and Canada.

Listening Task 2
Monday morning!

1. T: *Look at page 53.*

2. (**Optional**) Read the title: *"Monday morning!" What do you think this activity will be about?* Elicit answers from the students. (Answer: a schedule)

3. (**Optional**) If students find listening very difficult, do the Additional Support procedure below.

4. Read the instructions: *Listen. A secretary is taking telephone messages. Write the changes on the schedule.*

5. Play Listening Task 2 on the tape. Gesture for students to write the changes.

6. (**Optional**) To make sure students understand what to do, stop after the first two or three phone calls. Ask: *Who called? What time was his (her) appointment changed to?* As students answer, write the changes on the board or use an OHP transparency. Then play the rest of Listening Task 2.

7. If necessary, play Listening Task 2 a second time. Before replaying the tape, you may want to have students compare their answers in pairs. *Work with a partner. Look at your partner's answers. How many were the same? Then we'll listen again.*

8. Check by having students call out the changes. Write them on the board or use an OHP transparency. (Answers appear in blue on the opposite page.)

ADDITIONAL SUPPORT Have students read all the names on the schedule. Play the tape once. Have them put a check by each name they hear.

NOTES

• The secretary in a doctor's office is having a terrible day but is acting

professionally. The problems she is having are somewhat exaggerated.

• In North America, Monday morning has a negative image because people are returning to work after the weekend.

Your turn to talk

1. Divide the class into pairs. T: *What places or events could you invite a friend to?* As students answer, write the ideas on the board.

2. T: *Stand up and find a partner. Invite your partner to one of the places or events. Partner, flip a coin and give your answer. The _____ side of the coin means "yes." The _____ side means "no." If the answer is "yes," decide the time you will meet. If the answer is "no," give an excuse.*

3. Give students time to invite their partners.

4. T: *Change partners. Continue until you have invited 10 different people.*

5. Allow time for the activity. As students work, circulate and make sure they are deciding times or giving excuses.

6. (When most pairs have finished) T: *How many times did people accept your invitation?* You may wish to see which students' invitations were accepted most often.

NOTES

• If students are not familiar with flipping coins, demonstrate by putting the coin on your thumb and forefinger and moving your thumb up quickly. Let the students try. If some of them have difficulty, simply have them shake the coin in their hands and toss the coin onto a desk.

• Usually the "head" (front) side of the coin means "yes" and the "tail" (back) means "no." If the coins the students are using have established front and back sides, decide which will be front and back for the activity.

Monday morning!

❑ Listen. A secretary is taking telephone messages.
Write the changes on the schedule.

Monday, April 12

9:30	Call Ms. Park	2:00	↓
10:00	Ms. Riviera	2:30	Ms. Perry
10:30	Mr. ~~Long~~ Ms. Wells	3:00	Meeting with Dr. Chung
11:00	Mr. Black	3:30	Ms. Green
11:30	Mr. Long	4:00	Mr. Michaels
12:00	Mr. Rogers	4:30	Ms. Sato
12:30	~~Mr. Franks~~	5:00	HOSPITAL
1:00	LUNCH	5:30	
		Finally, cancel all appointments	
1:30	↓	6:00	↓

YOUR TURN TO TALK

As a full class, think of at least 10 places or events you could invite a friend to.
Then stand up and find a partner. Invite your partner to one of the places or events.
Partner, flip a coin and give your answer:

 = Say yes.
Decide the time.

 = Say no.
Give an excuse.

Change partners. Continue until you have invited 10 different people. How many
times did people accept your invitations?

Example

      A: Would you like to go to _____ on Saturday?

(Y) B: That sounds good. What time?

(or)(N)   Sorry, I'd really like to, but I have to work.

53

Youth culture

❑ Work with a partner.
Think about young people in your country.
What is popular with them?
How many things can you list for each topic?

SAMPLE ANSWERS

music _rock, especially musicians like..._

clothing _jeans, T-shirts, tennis shoes_

food _(names of local foods)_

free-time activities _camping, going to movies, eating out_

places _(names of local places)_

sports _skiing, tennis, soccer_

Youth culture

Topics/functions: Discussing the interests of young people, past and present
Listening skills: Identifying mistakes (Listening Task 1), understanding details (Listening Task 2)
Grammar/vocabulary: Past tenses: simple past and past progressive

Warming Up

1. Hold your book so that students can see page 54. T: *Look at page 54.*

2. Read the instructions:

Work with a partner.
Think about young people in your country.
What is popular with them?
How many things can you list for each topic?

3. (**Optional**) You may wish to do the first one or two items as a full class activity.

4. As students work, circulate and help pairs having difficulty.

5. (**Optional**) As some pairs finish, you may want to combine those pairs into groups of four. Have them compare answers.

6. Compare by having students call out ideas for each item. Students who had written the same answer raise their hands.

NOTES

• If your students are fairly young, this unit is a chance for them to be the "experts." Encourage them to provide more information and examples. Ask questions if you are interested.

• If your students are older, they can either base their answers on their images of young people or they can answer about the time when they themselves were teenagers.

• This unit contains both the simple past and the past progressive tenses. Their uses are different. The simple past is more common. It is used to talk about short, completed actions.

> The story started 200 years ago.
> He wore jeans.
> James Dean was a hero.

The past progressive uses *was/were* + verb + *-ing*. It is used to describe an action that was already happening.

> In the 1950s, rock and roll was getting popular.

Strategy exercise: *Looking for chances to practice*

As the course winds down, students should be encouraged to seek opportunities for practice outside of class. This can be made into a class project. Students can work in teams to find out the names of places where they can listen to or practice speaking English. This might include a list of favorite radio stations and any special programs they have, lists of upcoming movies or TV shows, or any supplementary books they could recommend.

Optional activities

(For use anytime during or after the unit.)

• *Top five.* Have students, working in pairs, agree on a list of the top five songs of the year (or of all time). If the titles are in their native language, they should translate them into English.

• *Time capsule.* Students work in small groups of four or five to make a "time capsule" of when they were teenagers. This capsule will be sealed and opened in fifty years. Students should make lists of things and people who were characteristic of the time.

Listening Task 1 Jeans

Note: The tapescript for Unit 17 begins on page T24.

1. T: *Look at page 55.*

2. (**Optional**) Read the title: *"Jeans." What do you think this activity will be about?* Elicit answers from the students. (Answer: the history of jeans)

3. (**Optional**) If students find listening very difficult, do the Additional Support procedure below.

4. Read the instructions: *Read this story.* (Allow time for students to read.)

5. T: *Now listen. There are 10 mistakes. The tape is correct. Find the mistakes. Write the correct information.*

6. Play Listening Task 1 on the tape. Gesture for students to write their answers.

7. (**Optional**) To make sure students understand what to do, stop after the first paragraph. Ask students: *What were the mistakes?*

8. If necessary, play Listening Task 1 a second time.

9. Check by having students call out the correct words. You may wish to use an OHP transparency. (Answers appear in blue on the opposite page.)

ADDITIONAL SUPPORT The first time you play the tape, students simply underline what they hear that is different from what is written. Then play the tape again and let them try to catch the specific information.

NOTES

• This task is somewhat unusual. In general, the students have not focused on every word. However, it is sometimes useful to do this. The "testing" nature of the task is softened by the content, which should be interesting, especially to younger students.

• If students read very slowly, encourage them to read the passage without using their dictionaries. They should skip over any words they don't know. If they feel there was a lot they didn't understand, have them go back and circle unknown words. Then, in pairs, they should try to guess the meaning based on the rest of the paragraph. Most students will do the guessing in their native language. Finally, they can look up the words in their dictionaries.

• This reading is based on an actual student composition which drew on information provided by the Levi-Strauss and Lee companies.

Culture corner

1. After students have read the Culture Corner, ask a few of them to answer the question: *What do people in your country like to spend money on?*

2. (**Optional**) After they have read the Culture Corner, have students work in groups of four or five. First, have them list all the types of entertainment mentioned in the reading. Then have them add at least two or three other things young people in their countries do for entertainment. Finally, ask them to see how many members in their group have done each activity in the past week (or month). Groups may wish to compare answers.

Jeans

❏ Read this story.
Now listen.
There are 10 mistakes. The tape is correct.
Find the mistakes. Write the correct information.

Jeans: The "Uniform" of Youth

Jeans are very popular with young people all over the
world
~~United States~~. Some people say that jeans are the

"uniform" of youth. But they haven't always been ~~blue~~.
popular

The story of jeans started almost 200 years ago. People

in Genoa, Italy, made pants. The cloth made in Genoa was

called "jeanos." The pants were called "jeans." In 1850, a

salesman in California began selling pants made of canvas.

His name was Levi Strauss. Because they were so strong,

"Levi's pants" became popular with gold miners, farmers,
cowboys
and ~~students~~. Six years later, Levi began making his pants

with a blue cotton cloth called denim. Soon after, factory
Europe
workers in the United States and ~~Asia~~ began wearing jeans.

Young people usually didn't wear them.

In the 1950s, two people helped make jeans popular

with teenagers: Elvis Presley, the king of rock and roll,
movie
and James Dean, a famous ~~TV~~ star. Elvis wore tight jeans.

music
Most parents didn't like Elvis or his ~~jeans~~. But teenagers

loved him and started to dress like him. In *Rebel Without*

a Cause, James Dean wore jeans. He was a hero to many

young people.

During the 1960s, rock and roll became even more
freedom
popular. Young people had more ~~money~~. Their clothes

showed their independence. Some people decorated their
flowers
jeans with colorful patches and ~~designs~~.

In the '70s and '80s, jeans became very expensive. In

addition to the regular brands like Levi's and Lee,

famous designers like Calvin Klein and Pierre Cardin

began making "designer jeans." They were very stylish
expensive
and very ~~fashionable~~.

20
Jeans are so popular that Levi's has sold over ~~10~~

billion pairs. Almost anywhere in the world you know

what young people want to wear: jeans!

Young people in most countries are interested in entertainment. In the United
States and Canada, people under 25 spend about 6 percent of their income on
entertainment. Of that money, about one-third is used for tickets for movies,
concerts, and other events. A little more than one-third is used for things like
stereos, video players, and televisions. Reading is also popular. Young people
spend nearly 10 percent of their entertainment income on books and magazines.
What do young people in your country like to spend money on?

Rock and roll!

❏ Look at the covers of the CDs.
Do you know anything about these types of popular music?

❏ Listen. A music expert is talking about the history of popular music.
When did each type of music become popular? Write the dates on the lines.
Write one or more facts about each type.

mid-1950s

popular on radio

early 1960s

black performers
Detroit

mid-1960s

Beatles
Rolling Stones
London

mid-1970s

rock fans hated

late 1970s

London
New York

early 1980s

leather clothes
parents hated it

mid-1980s

slang
popular all over the
world

early 1990s

Africa
Brazil
different languages

YOUR TURN TO TALK

Think about young people in your country. Do they often disagree with their
parents? What kinds of things do parents and young people disagree about? Write
five ideas. Then work in groups of five. Combine lists. Which ideas are the same?
Which are different?

56

Listening Task 2 Rock and roll!

Listening skill: Understanding details

1. T: Look at page 56.

2. (**Optional**) Read the title: *"Rock and roll." What do you think this activity will be about?* Elicit answers from the students. (Answer: a history of rock and roll music)

3. Read the first part of the instructions: *Look at the covers of the CDs. Do you know anything about these types of popular music?* Allow time for students to answer. They can do this either by saying or writing their answers. You many prefer to do this activity in pairs or small groups.

4. (**Optional**) If students find listening very difficult, do the Additional Support procedure.

5. Read the rest of the instructions. *Listen. A music expert is talking about the history of popular music. When did each type of music become popular? Write the dates on the lines. Write one or more facts about each type.*

6. Play Listening Task 2 on the tape. Gesture for students to write the dates and extra facts.

7. (**Optional**) To make sure students understand what to do, stop after the speaker talks about Motown. Ask students: *When did Motown become popular? What else did you hear about it?* Then play the rest of Listening Task 2.

8. If necessary, play Listening Task 2 a second time. Before replaying the tape, you may want to have students compare their answers in pairs. T: *Work with a partner. Look at your partner's answers. How many were the same? Then we'll listen again.*

9. Check by having students call out their answers. Write the answers on the board. (Answers appear in blue on the opposite page.)

ADDITIONAL SUPPORT Before they listen, have students work in groups of three or four. They should look at the CD covers and should write as many things as they know about each type of music. The most commonly known information will be the names of musicians, groups, and songs. If there are types of music that students aren't familiar with, they should write at least one question about each. (You may wish to have them do the listening activity in pairs.)

NOTES

• Although a teacher may not be a fan of rock and roll, it is often very popular with students. Also, the radio can provide a great source of listening practice. Since students may be more knowledgeable on the topic than the teacher, encourage them to add information they know about each type of music.

• The name *Motown* comes from the nickname for Detroit ("Motor Town"), the automobile manufacturing capital of the United States.

Your turn to talk

1. T: *Think about young people in your country. Do they often disagree with their parents? What kinds of things do parents and young people disagree about? Write five ideas.* Allow time for students to make their lists.

2. T: *Now work in groups of five. Combine lists. Which ideas are the same? Which are different?*

3. After five or ten minutes, you may wish to elicit the most common ideas or ideas they disagreed on. List them on the board and see if other groups discussed those items.

   Note: If you have students of very different ages, it is often interesting to have them work together on this activity to get different opinions.

UNIT 18
Making a difference

> ***Topics/functions:*** Discussing environmental issues
> ***Listening skills:*** Understanding explanations (Listening Task 1), understanding details (Listening Task 2)
> ***Grammar/vocabulary:*** Simple present, infinitive of purpose (*You use it to . . .*)

Warming Up

1. Hold your book so that students can see page 57. T: *Look at page 57.*

2. Read the instructions:

> *Work with a partner.*
> *What can people do to help save energy and stop pollution?*
> *How many things can you think of?*
> *Write them.*

3. (**Optional**) You may want to do the first one as a full group activity to make sure everyone understands what to do.

4. T: *Which things do you usually do? Circle them.*

5. As students work, circulate and help pairs having difficulty. Check their understanding by asking questions such as these: *What can people do to save electricity? How can people make less garbage?*

6. After most pairs have written ideas for all the items, you may want to have students call out their ideas as you list them on the board.

NOTES

• Worldwide interest in and knowledge of environmental issues is growing. It may be interesting for students to compare the things they do now to those they did a few years ago.

• The topic of the environment is best approached matter-of-factly. The students' interest should govern the discussion.

Strategy exercise: *Self-monitoring/ evaluation*

The most successful learners learn to monitor their own mistakes, but they also know when they are monitoring too much. Now might be a good time for students, either individually or collectively, to decide their next step in language learning (the things they still need to work on). They should then decide which ones are important and which are not.

Optional activities

(For use anytime during or after the unit.)

• ***Improving the school.*** What things can be done at school to protect the environment? Have students work in small groups to make a list. Then have them join another group and pick the three best ideas.

• ***A picture is worth a thousand words.*** Have students, working in pairs, make a poster about an environmental issue. The poster should suggest a change in behavior that would help the environment. For example, "Drive to work in carpools."

Making a difference

❑ Work with a partner.
What can people do to help save energy and stop pollution?
How many things can you think of?
Write them.

SAMPLE ANSWERS

	To save electricity? *Turn off the lights when they are not in use.*
	To save trees? *Recycle paper.*
	To save gasoline? *Use public transportation and buy smaller cars.*
	To make less garbage? *Recycle cans and bottles.*

❑ Which things do you usually do?
Circle them.

Little things help.

❑ Look at the pictures. What could you do with these things to help the earth?

❑ Now listen. People are talking about improving the environment.
What do they do with these things? Fill in the blanks.

1. newspapers

Recycle them.

2. cups

Don't use Styrofoam cups.

3. bags

Use cloth bags instead of
paper or _plastic_ bags.

4. plastic bottles

Use in the _toilet_
tank to save water.

5. an air pressure gauge

Check _tires_ ; it saves
gasoline .

These are things people in the United States do to help the environment.

	Regularly	Sometimes	Never
Recycle cans and bottles	64%	19%	17%
Buy environmentally safe products	53	31	15
Recycle newspapers	50	14	36
Buy recycled products	47	30	22
Give money to environmental groups	18	30	51
Carpool (share rides) to work/school	17	12	70

What kinds of things do you do in your country?

Listening Task 1
Little things help

Note: The tapescript for Unit 18 begins on page T25.

1. T: *Look at page 58.*

2. (**Optional**) Read the title: *"Little things help." What do you think this activity will be about?* Elicit answers from the students. (Answer: small things that can help the environment)

3. (**Optional**) If students find listening very difficult, do the Additional Support procedure.

4. Read the first part of the instructions: *Look at the pictures. What could you do with these things to help the earth?* Allow students time to write or say their ideas. You may wish to have them do this step in pairs.

5. Read the rest of the instructions: *Now listen. People are talking about improving the environment. What do they do with these things? Fill in the blanks.*

6. Play Listening Task 1 on the tape. Gesture for students to write their answers.

7. (**Optional**) To make sure students understand what to do, stop after number two. Have students say what they wrote. Then play the rest of Listening Task 1.

8. If necessary, play Listening Task 1 a second time.

9. Check by having students say their answers. Write them on the board. (Answers appear in blue on the opposite page.)

ADDITIONAL SUPPORT Have students close their books. Write the following words on the board:

> air gauge
> bags
> cups
> newspapers
> plastic bottles

Play the tape once. Have students try to understand which item is being discussed. If possible, they should also try to catch one or two bits of information from each section.

NOTES

• If you feel that students need more background information about these items, in particular the air pressure gauge, it is best to wait until they have heard the tape. It explains the uses of the things.

• Students in countries such as Japan and Australia, where toilets often have a handle which controls the amounts of water used, may be interested to know that such devices are unusual in North America.

• Information in this task is from *50 Simple Things You Can Do to Save the Earth*, by The Earthworks Group, Box 25, 1400 Shattuck Avenue, Berkeley, CA 94709 USA.

Culture corner

1. After students have read the Culture Corner, have them work in small groups to compare answers to the question: *What kinds of things do you do in your country?*

2. (**Optional**) After reading the Culture Corner, have students conduct their own poll. Ask them to stand and find a partner. Then have them ask their partner each of the items, preceding it with "How often do you . . . ?" They record their partner's responses. Then have students change partners and continue until they have asked all six questions to at least five people. It may be interesting to poll the entire class at the end to see how students' answers compare to the information in the chart.

Listening Task 2 Recycling

1. T: *Look at page 59.*

2. (**Optional**) Read the title: *Recycling.*

3. Read the instructions: *Listen to this radio announcement. How much of these materials do people in the United States use? Fill in the blanks.*

4. Play Listening Task 2 on the tape. Gesture for students to write their answers.

5. (**Optional**) If students find listening very difficult, do the Additional Support procedure below.

6. (**Optional**) To make sure students understand what to do, stop after the first two or three items and have students say their answers. Then play the rest of Listening Task 2.

7. If necessary, play Listening Task 2 a second time. Before replaying the tape, you may want to have students compare their answers in pairs. T: *Work with a partner. Look at your partner's answers. How many were the same? Then we'll listen again.*

8. Check by having students call out their answers. Write them on the board or use an OHP transparency. (Answers appear in blue on the opposite page.)

ADDITIONAL SUPPORT Have students do the activity in pairs. Also, stop the tape between items to give them time to think, check with each other, and write.

NOTES

• Information in this task is from the Environmental Defense Fund, 1616 P Street, N.W., Washington, DC 20077 USA.

• Listening Task 2 is in the style of a radio public service announcement (PSA). PSAs are commercials for non-profit organizations played by radio stations.

Such PSAs, when relevant, are a good source of extra listening practice.

Your turn to talk

1. T: *What things do you do to help the environment? What do other people do? What do you wish more people would do? What other issues are you interested in? Social issues? Local issues?*

2. Whether students answer these questions in a whole group will depend on the students. If you are only having them think about the topic before the speaking activity, allow time for them to think and organize their ideas.

3. T: *Work with a partner. Discuss your ideas for one minute.*

4. (after one minute) T: *Stop. Change partners. Discuss your ideas with another partner.*

5. Continue as long as student interest is maintained.

   Note: An efficient way to organize the activity is to have the students stand in lines facing each other. When it is time to change partners, everyone moves one person to the right. The person at the end of the line comes to the front of the line.

LISTENING TASK 2

Recycling

❑ Listen to this radio announcement.
How much of these materials do people in the United States use?
Fill in the blanks.

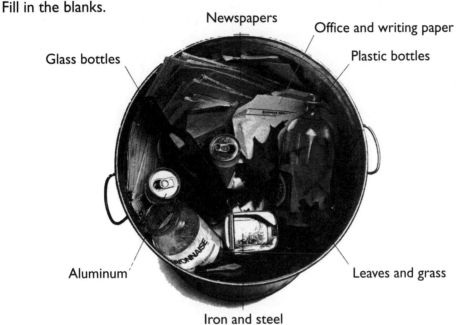

Newspapers

Office and writing paper

Glass bottles

Plastic bottles

Aluminum

Leaves and grass

Iron and steel

aluminum: enough to rebuild all *commercial airplanes* every three months

iron and steel: enough to supply all of our *car (automobile)* makers

newspapers: *500,000* trees a week

office and writing paper: enough to build a wall from *Los Angeles* to *New York*

leaves and grass: *24 million* tons each year

glass: enough to fill *the two tallest* buildings in New York City every two weeks

plastic: *2½ million* plastic bottles every hour

YOUR TURN TO TALK

What things do you do to help the environment? What do other people do? What do you wish more people would do? What other issues are you interested in? Social issues? Local issues? Work with a partner. Discuss your ideas for one minute. Then change partners. Discuss your ideas with your new partner.

It's in the news.

❑ Work with a partner.
Think about recent news stories.
What is the most important news story for each topic?
Write your answers.
Write extra facts about one news story.

	News Story	Extra Facts
International news		
National news		
Local news		
Sports		
Music, art, or science		

LEADERS OPEN TALKS IN QUEBEC

Mayor backs new plan

Scientists find new cure

STUDENTS STAGE PROTEST

Soccer finals to be played in Spain

UN HELPS AID EFFORTS

U N I T   1 9

It's in the news.

> **Topics/functions:** Discussing current events
> **Listening skills:** Understanding topics
> (Listening Task 1), understanding
> details (Listening Task 2)
> **Grammar/vocabulary:** Past tenses: simple
> past and past progressive

Warming Up

1. Hold your book so that students can see page 60. T: *Look at page 60.*

2. Read the instructions:

> *Work with a partner. Think about recent news stories.*
> *What is the most important news story for each topic?*
> *Write your answers. Write extra facts about one news story.*

You may want to do a few examples as a full group to remind students of current news stories.

3. As students work, circulate and help pairs having difficulty. Check their understanding by asking questions like these:

> *What are the big stories in the news?*
> *What else do you know about that?*

4. Compare answers by having students call out news story topics. Have other pairs who listed the same topics raise their hands.

NOTES

• You know best what to expect from your students. Some classes will be able to easily add details about current news while other groups will find it more difficult.

• If any pairs are unable to think of a story for one of the topics, have them list a story for a different topic.

Strategy exercise: *Linking learning with the world*

This unit gives students another opportunity to think about how much they know about the world outside the classroom and how they can use that knowledge in the classroom. Students can prepare a "typical" newscast for the week. Which stories have continued? What words have been repeated? Alternatively, they can listen to a news story and find a newspaper article about the same story, listing the things that are the same.

Optional activities

(For use anytime during or after the unit.)

• ***Person of the year.*** Have students work in small groups to choose the person of the year for the world or their country. They should give reasons. Then have them join another group (with a different candidate) and argue for their choice.

• ***Headline hunt.*** Obtain copies of English language newspapers. Have students work in pairs. Give each pair a newspaper or a few pages from one. Ask students to scan the headlines, looking for any new or unusual words. They read the news story and try to guess the meanings. Finally, write the words on the board; discuss or explain them as needed.

Listening Task 1
What are they talking about?

Note: The tapescript for Unit 19 begins on page T26.

1. T: *Look at page 61.*

2. (**Optional**) Read the title: *"What are they talking about?" What do you think this activity will be about?* Elicit answers from the students. (Answer: topics of news stories)

3. (**Optional**) If students find listening very difficult, do the Additional Support procedure below.

4. Read the instructions: *Listen. People are talking about newspaper articles. What is the order of the stories? Number the pictures. Write extra facts about each story. There are two extra pictures.*

5. Play Listening Task 1 on the tape. Gesture for students to write their answers.

6. (**Optional**) To make sure students understand what to do, stop after the second one. Ask students: *Which picture is number two? What extra facts did you write?* Then play the rest of Listening Task 1.

7. If necessary, play Listening Task 1 a second time.

8. Check by drawing six squares on the board, one to represent each picture. Have students say the order of the pictures and the extra facts as you write them. (Answers appear in blue on the opposite page.)

ADDITIONAL SUPPORT Have students, working in pairs, look at each picture and try to write at least three words about it. This activity makes students more familiar with the pictures and gets them thinking about likely topics.

NOTES

• The stories in this task and in Listening Task 2 are fictitious (except for the story about the locked out pilot), but are based on recurring kinds of news items.

Culture corner

1. After they have read the Culture Corner, ask a few students to answer the question: *What is difficult to understand in newspapers in your country?*

2. (**Optional**) After students have read the Culture Corner, have them go back to the news items they wrote on page 60. Remind them that newspaper headlines are always short. Then ask them to try to give as much information in as few words as possible. In pairs, have students try to write one short and clear headline for each news item. They may use the special vocabulary presented, but they don't have to. A variation is for you to specify one item for each category by either telling the students, or eliciting suggestions from the class. Pairs then compete to write the shortest, clearest headlines.

What are they talking about?

❏ Listen. People are talking about newspaper articles.
What is the order of the stories?
Number the pictures (1– 4). Write extra facts about each story.
There are two extra pictures.

2

trade meeting in Paris
disagreement about farm
   imports

_____
_____
_____

_____
_____
_____

1

rock musician running
   for mayor

3

Bulldogs beat Wildcats
_____

4

pilot locked out of plane
_____

CULTURE CORNER

Headlines in English language newspapers can be difficult to understand. Headlines usually are not in complete sentences. Short words like "a," an," "the," and the verb "to be" aren't usually used. Sometimes special words are used to save space. These are some common ones (with their meanings):

head (leader)
hit (criticize or affect badly)
key (important)

push or back (support or encourage)
talks (negotiations)

Examples
Agency head pushes peace talks = The leader of an agency encourages peace negotiations.
Key trade plan hit = An important trade plan is criticized.

What is difficult to understand in newspapers in your language?

The six o'clock news

❏ Read these newspaper stories.
Then listen to the news on the radio.
Write the missing information.
The type of information you need is in [blue].

1.

COUNTRIES ARGUE FARM PRODUCT IMPORTS

[City] *Paris* – The leaders of the seven major industrialized nations met today to discuss trade problems. The key issue is imported agricultural products. Nearly half of the countries attending the Paris conference are protesting pressure to open their markets to foreign farm products, especially [type] *beef* . Little progress is expected to be made in this area. Several leaders are facing elections this year and farm voters are demanding protection.

2.

Rock star runs for mayor

[City] *San Francisco* – Rock star Jerry Ward announced today that he is entering the mayor's race. Ward hopes to use his popularity as well as his public support of striking [type] *hospital* workers to make up for his late start in the elections. Ward says he knows what the people want because rock is the music of the people. His campaign slogan is "From concert hall to City Hall, Jerry's with you."

3.

Bulldogs down Wildcats

Vancouver – The Vancouver Bulldogs beat the Portland Wildcats [game score] *11* to *1* Tuesday night.

The winning pitcher was Juan Sanchez. It was his second win of the season. Bryce pitched for the Wildcats. The Bulldogs are the only team that hasn't lost this season. They will play the San José [team] *Lions* tomorrow.

4.

Airline pilot locked out

[City] *New York* – Passengers on Transglobal Airlines flight [number] *65* , while waiting for take-off at the airport, were surprised by a loud banging on the plane's door. When the crew checked, they found the plane's pilot, who had been locked out.

YOUR TURN TO TALK

Work in groups of three. You are radio news announcers. Think of a recent news story that most people know about. First practice telling the story. Then change groups. Tell your story to your new group. Partners, listen. Option: Change three or more facts in the news story. Partners, try to find the changes.

Listening Task 2
The six o'clock news

Listening skill: Understanding details

1. T: *Look at page 62.*

2. (**Optional**) Read the title: *"The six o'clock news." What do you think this activity will be about?* Elicit answers from the students. (Answer: a radio news broadcast)

3. Read the first part of the instructions: *Read these newspaper stories.* Allow time for the students to read.

4. (**Optional**) If students find listening very difficult, do the Additional Support procedure below.

5. Read the rest of the instructions: *Then listen to the news on the radio. Write the missing information. The type of information you need is in blue.*

6. Play Listening Task 2 on the tape. Gesture for students to write the missing information.

7. (**Optional**) To make sure students understand what to do, stop after the first story. Ask: *What did you write in the second blank?* Then play the rest of Listening Task 2.

8. If necessary, play Listening Task 2 a second time. Before replaying the tape, you may want to have students compare their answers in pairs. T: *Work with a partner. Look at your partner's answers. How many are the same? Then we'll listen again.*

9. Check by having students call out their answers. (Answers appear in blue on the opposite page.)

ADDITIONAL SUPPORT Tell students that the stories they will hear are similar to the stories in Listening Task 1. Make sure they have adequate time in step 3 to read the stories. As they listen, pause the tape after every two or three sentences to give students time to think.

NOTES

• The radio script does not follow the newspaper stories exactly. The ideas are in the same order but the wording is different. This is to help students listen and scan at the same time.

• Most radio stations in North America have regular news broadcasts. Generally they begin on the hour (six o'clock, eight o'clock, etc.) Although most radio stations broadcast locally, many are members of networks and broadcast regular national reports.

Your turn to talk

1. Divide the class into groups of three. T: *Work in groups of three. You are radio news announcers. Think of a recent news story that most people know about. First, practice telling the story.*

2. As they work, circulate and help. Students may want to write notes about the story but encourage them not to write it out completely.

3. T: *Now change groups. Tell your story to your new groups. Partners, listen.*

Note: Decide if you want the students to use the option of changing facts in the story. This is a useful option since it increases interest and the partners' reason for listening. The results are often quite creative.

UNIT 20
Dreams and screams

Topic/function: Telling an unusual story
Listening skills: Understanding details
  (Listening Task 1), understanding and
  enjoying a story (Listening Task 2)
Grammar/vocabulary: Past tenses: simple
  past and past progressive; sequence
  markers

Warming Up

1. Hold your book so that students can see page 63. T: *Look at page 63.*

2. Read the instructions:
  Are you afraid of these things?
  Check your answers.
  Gesture for students to check.

3. (Decide the number of students you want in each group.) T: *Work in a group of six to ten people. Compare answers. Which things are the scariest to your group?*

4. As students work, circulate and help groups having difficulty.

5. You may wish to poll students at the end to see which things students find the scariest. Do this by having groups report or by reading out each item and having students raise their hands if they are afraid of them.

NOTES

• Encourage an atmosphere of fun. Nearly everyone has some fears that aren't very rational. Let students laugh at themselves.

Strategy exercise: *Summarizing*

As homework, have students watch a video or TV program in English, or listen to an English song or radio broadcast. Ask them to write a summary of what they heard and share it with their peers in groups. They should prepare a list of new words that their peers might not know.

Optional activity

(For use anytime during or after the unit.)

• *Scary things.* Have students work in pairs. If a class is multicultural, students from different countries should share what ghosts do and what they look like in their countries. Are there monsters that are unique to their countries? When do they appear? If the class is monocultural, they should list as many local legends as they can.

Dreams and screams

❑ Are you afraid of these things?
Check (✔) your answers.

	Yes	A little	Not at all
spiders	☐	☐	☐
high places	☐	☐	☐
snakes	☐	☐	☐
big dogs	☐	☐	☐
storms/thunder	☐	☐	☐
dark, lonely roads	☐	☐	☐
airplanes	☐	☐	☐
the ocean	☐	☐	☐
going to the dentist	☐	☐	☐

❑ Work in a group of 6–10 people.
Compare answers.
Which things are the scariest to your group?

That's strange.

❑ Listen to two stories about unusual creatures.
Write three or more facts about each story.

I. Space creatures   *SAMPLE ANSWERS*

short: 125 centimeters (4 feet)
large heads with no hair
faces like frogs
may be green

2. The Loch Ness monster

Loch Ness: lake in Scotland
plays in the water (lake)
looks like a dinosaur
long neck, small head

©SAM
VIVIANO
1993

❑ Do you think UFOs and space creatures are real?   Yes ☐   No ☐

Do you believe in the Loch Ness monster?   Yes ☐   No ☐

CULTURE
CORNER

Many cultures have "monsters." Asian and European cultures have stories about dragons. In both cultures, dragons guard the doors to places full of riches (money and gold). Pictures of dragons are often painted on doors and gates. In Europe, the dragons never give their money away. In Asia, dragons often give presents. The Western dragon is evil, but the Eastern dragon can be kind and is a symbol of luck. In European cultures, dragons usually live alone. In Asian cultures, they live together in societies. What monsters do you tell stories about in your country?

Listening Task I That's strange.

Note: The tapescript for Unit 20 begins on page T27.

I. T: *Look at page 64.*

2. (Optional) Read the title: *"That's strange." What do you think this activity will be about?* Elicit answers from the students. (Answer: space creatures and the Loch Ness monster)

3. (Optional) If students find listening very difficult, do the Additional Support procedure below.

4. Read the instructions: *Listen to two stories about unusual creatures. Write three or more facts about each story.*

5. Play Listening Task 1 on the tape. Gesture for students to write their answers.

6. (Optional) Point out that students don't need to write full sentences. Taking short notes is enough. You may want to stop the tape after the first story to check. Then play the rest of Listening Task 1.

7. If necessary, play Listening Task 1 a second time.

8. Check by having students say what they wrote. Write or draw it on the board. Have students raise their hands to show whether they believe in the creatures. (Answers appear in blue on the opposite page.)

ADDITIONAL SUPPORT Tell students that they will hear about space creatures and the Loch Ness monster. Have students, working in groups of two to four, think of at least three things they want to know about each. The class may want to discuss their questions as a group before listening to the tape.

NOTES

• Whether or not these creatures are real is beside the point. People have talked about these creatures for a long time and they are interesting to students.

• Unidentified Flying Objects (UFOs) technically refer to anything which is flying and is not identified. In daily conversation, however, a UFO is assumed to be a spacecraft from another planet. Note that in English the letters are pronounced separately (U-F-O) not as a word (Ufo).

• Some students may be more familiar with the Loch Ness monster by its nickname, Nessie.

Culture corner

I. After students have read the Culture Corner, have small groups compare answers to the question: *What monsters do you tell stories about in your country?*

2. (Optional) Make copies of the following paragraph. You will need one copy for each pair of students. Before students read the Culture Corner in their books, have them work in pairs. They read the paragraph and guess what the missing words are. Then they check their books to see if they were correct. Words with a similar meaning are OK. (For example, the first blank could easily be *doors, entrances, gates,* etc.)

Many cultures have monsters. Asian and European cultures have stories about dragons. In both cultures, dragons guard the _____ to places full of riches (money and gold). Pictures of dragons are often _____ on doors and gates. In Europe, the dragons never give their _____ away. In Asia, dragons often give presents. The Western dragon is _____ , but the Eastern dragon can be kind and is a symbol of luck. In European cultures, dragons usually live alone. In Asian cultures, they live _____ in societies.

Listening Task 2
Wait until the master comes.

Listening skill: Understanding and enjoying a story

1. T: *Look at page 65.*

2. (**Optional**) Read the title: *"Wait until the master comes." What do you think this activity will be about?* Elicit answers from the students. (Answer: a scary story)

3. Read the first part of the instructions: *Look at the words and pictures. What do you think the story is about?* Give students time to read the words and answer, either in small groups or as a whole class.

4. Read the next instruction: *Listen to the story.* Play the Listening Task 2 story.

5. (**Optional**) If students find listening very difficult, do the Additional Support procedure below.

6. See the variation suggested in the first item, under Notes.

7. If necessary, play Listening Task 2 a second time. You may want to have all students discuss their understanding of it before the second listening. Also, you may want to stop the tape a little before the end.

8. Finish by having students raise their hands to indicate whether or not they liked it and whether or not it was scary.

ADDITIONAL SUPPORT As they listen, have students point to the words they see at the time they hear them. You may want to pause the tape after each printed word or phrase to give them time to think.

NOTES

• **Variation:** Stop the tape just before the old man jumps out of the window. Have students work in pairs or small groups to predict how the story will end. Then have them share their endings.

• Encourage students to enjoy this story. It is designed to create an emotional reaction. Some teachers even add to the atmosphere by turning down the lights in the classroom.

• Teachers are sometimes surprised by the unusually open-ended nature of the task. Remember, the students deciding whether or not they like something actually show a very sophisticated level of understanding. They process not only the meaning but their emotional reactions as well.

• This story is based on a folk tale from the southern part of the United States.

Your turn to talk

1. Divide the class into groups of four. T: *Work in groups of four. Did you like "Wait Until the Master Comes"? Was it scary? Everyone, give an opinion. Tell why you did or didn't think it was scary.*

2. Give students time to give their opinions.

3. (after a few minutes) T: *Now, each person tell a story. It can be one you know or one you make up.*

4. (**Optional**) You may want to give students time to write a story outline similar to the list on the student's page.

5. Give students time to tell their stories.

   Variation: Have students choose a well known folk or fairy tale, but make three or more changes in the story. Partners listen for the changes.

Wait until the master comes.

❏ Look at the words and pictures.
What do you think the story is about?

❏ Listen to the story.

old man
the woods
got lost
old house
rain
made a fire
sleep
a cat
another cat
"Shall we do it now?"
"Wait until the master comes."
a larger cat
the fourth cat
in front of the door
"It's almost time."
window
runs
"At last, I'm safe!"

❏ Did you like this story?   Yes ☐   No ☐

   Was it scary?   Yes ☐   No ☐

YOUR TURN TO TALK

Work in groups of four. Did you like "Wait Until the Master Comes"? Was it scary? Everyone, give an opinion. Tell why or why not. Then each person tells a story. It can be one you know or one you make up.

World map

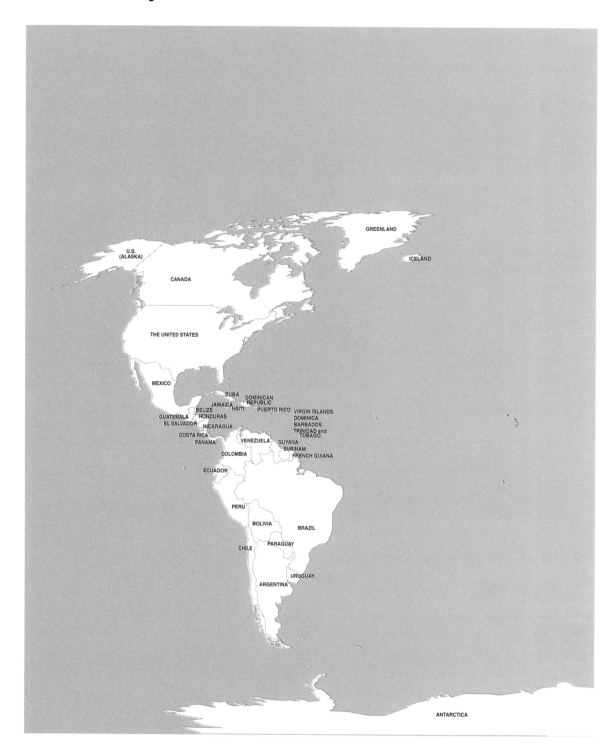

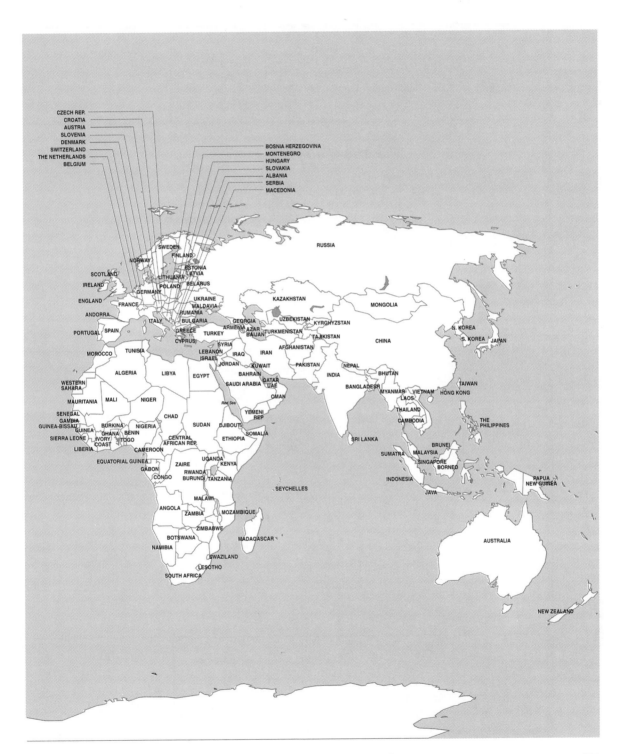

CZECH REP.
CROATIA
AUSTRIA
SLOVENIA
DENMARK
SWITZERLAND
THE NETHERLANDS
BELGIUM

BOSNIA HERZEGOVINA
MONTENEGRO
HUNGARY
SLOVAKIA
ALBANIA
SERBIA
MACEDONIA

RUSSIA

SWEDEN
FINLAND
NORWAY
ESTONIA
LATVIA
SCOTLAND
LITHUANIA
BELARUS
IRELAND
GERMANY
POLAND
ENGLAND
FRANCE
UKRAINE
ANDORRA
MALDAVIA
RUMANIA
ITALY
BULGARIA
GEORGIA
PORTUGAL
SPAIN
GREECE
ARMENIA
AZAR
BAIJAN
CYPRUS
TURKEY

KAZAKHSTAN

MONGOLIA

UZBEKISTAN
KYRGHYZSTAN
N. KOREA
TURKMENISTAN
S. KOREA
JAPAN
TAJIKISTAN
CHINA
SYRIA
LEBANON
IRAN
AFGHANISTAN
ISRAEL
IRAQ
MOROCCO
TUNISIA
JORDAN
KUWAIT
PAKISTAN
NEPAL
BHUTAN
WESTERN
SAHARA
ALGERIA
LIBYA
EGYPT
BAHRAIN
QATAR
SAUDI ARABIA
UAE
INDIA
TAIWAN
MAURITANIA
MALI
NIGER
OMAN
BANGLADESH
MYANMAR
VIETNAM
HONG KONG
Red Sea
LAOS
SENEGAL
YEMENI
REP
THAILAND
GAMBIA
BURKINA
NIGERIA
CHAD
SUDAN
DJIBOUTI
CAMBODIA
GUINEA-BISSAU
GUINEA
GHANA
BENIN
THE
PHILIPPINES
SIERRA LEONE
IVORY
TOGO
CENTRAL
SOMALIA
COAST
AFRICAN REP.
ETHIOPIA
SRI LANKA
BRUNEI
LIBERIA
CAMEROON
SUMATRA
MALAYSIA
EQUATORIAL GUINEA
ZAIRE
UGANDA
SINGAPORE
GABON
KENYA
BORNEO
RWANDA
CONGO
BURUNDI
TANZANIA
SEYCHELLES
INDONESIA
PAPUA
NEW GUINEA
JAVA
MALAWI
ANGOLA
ZAMBIA
MOZAMBIQUE
AUSTRALIA
ZIMBABWE
BOTSWANA
MADAGASCAR
NAMIBIA
SWAZILAND
LESOTHO
SOUTH AFRICA

NEW ZEALAND

The teaching procedure for this activity appears on page T29.

| Start here ➡ | What are you going to do next weekend? | Tell about your best friend. | What free-time activities do you like? | What 3 foods are most typical of your country? |

What is the most important recent news story?

Tell about a vacation you'd like to take. ✈

What is a rule that many people don't follow?

Who do you respect?

Do you want to change anything about the way you look? What is it?

The *Activation* game

- Work in groups of 3 or 4.
- Each player needs a place marker.
- Put the marker on "Start here."
- Close your eyes. Touch the "How many spaces?" box with a pencil. Move that many spaces.
- Read the sentence(s). Answer with at least 3 things.
- Each partner asks one question about what you said.
- When you land on a TEAMWORK space, everyone answers.
- If someone else lands on the same TEAMWORK space, any player can ask that person a question.
- Take turns.

| TEAMWORK Each person says a number larger than 1,000. Then everyone tries to add all the numbers. Who is the fastest? • Do this 3 times. | What do you do that makes the world better? | What don't you like shopping for? |
| | What job around the house do you hate to do? ☹ | ??????????? Any player can ask you one question. ??????????? |

| Have you ever been very sick? When? What did you do? | ??????????? You can ask one question to any player. ??????????? | Do you know a scary story? What is it about? | Tell about an English lesson where you learned a lot. | TEAMWORK What do you do (or should you do) to help the environment? |

| Give directions to your favorite restaurant. | Tell about a food you liked when you were a child. | What is your favorite kind of music? ♪ 𝄞 ♫ | What do you enjoy shopping for? | **TEAMWORK** How many gestures can you think of in 1 minute? Say what they mean. |

| What is the most difficult part of learning English? |

| **TEAMWORK** How many gestures can you think of in 1 minute? Say what they mean. |

How many spaces?

2	1	3	1	3	2
1	3	4	2	3	1
3	1	2	1	2	3
1	2	1	3	5	2
3	5	2	1	2	3
2	1	3	4	3	1

Tell about something you didn't need but bought anyway.

Tell about a time you felt really good.

What do your parents look like?

| What rule or law don't you like? | What is (or was) your favorite subject in school? | What is the most exciting job in the world? | ??????????? You can ask one question to any player. ??????????? | **TEAMWORK** How many things do you have with you that are from other countries? |

| Tell about something that happened while you were traveling. | What do you do on Sundays? | Can you tell a story or joke in English? | Do you know a gesture from another country? What is it? | **TEAMWORK** What do you do for your health? List as many things as you can in 1 minute. |

| What do you like about another culture? | Give directions to a place you like. | ??????????? Any player can ask you one question. ??????????? | What job around the house should you do today? Will you? | What is your favorite way to get the news? |

The world market: game leader

WARMING UP

❏ You are the game leader.
Ask the questions and keep score.
Your partners will guess the answers. (They use page 27.)

Example
Leader: What country's biggest export is rice?
Student 1: China.
Leader: No, that's not right.
Student 2: Thailand.
Leader: That's right. You get one point.

EXPORT CHALLENGE

Look at the products. Each product is the biggest export of one of these countries:

Australia	the Bahamas	Canada	China
France	India	Italy	Mexico
Norway	the Philippines	Spain	Thailand

Take turns. Guess the country which sells more of each product than any other product. (Cross out the country after a correct guess. There are two extra countries listed.)

PRODUCTS:

1. rice *Thailand*

2. beef *Australia*

3. wheat *Canada*

4. oil *Norway*

5. cotton *Mexico*

6. clothing and cloth
France

7. fruit *Spain*

8. diamonds *India*

9. lobster *the Bahamas*

10. electronic equipment
the Philippines

Each correct answer = 1 point.
Your points: _____

Tapescript

The following tapescript, which includes all of the listening tasks in the text, reflects *Active Listening*'s emphasis on natural, spoken English. There are, of course, differences between spoken and written English. This is a transcription of the spoken language.

You may occasionally want students to see the tapescript. For that reason, permission is granted to photocopy the script. However, the authors strongly suggest that this be done only occasionally and for specific reasons. Many students are too "word-level dependent." That is, they rely on trying overall meaning. If they insist on reading along with the script for every lesson, it can actually hurt their ability to listen and understand.

Here are two examples of situations where you might want to give out copies of the script:
• After students have completed the tasks in their text, you may want them to go back and note the uses of a particular grammatical form. In that case, you might give out the script and play the tape again, having them underline the times the form is used.

• If a class found a particular listening segment extremely difficult, you may want to give them a copy of the script. Have them read along silently as you play the tape. This increases their reading speed as well as letting them combine reading with listening to understand the segment. Then have them put away the script. Play the tape again and let them see how much they understood.

Before you begin: An introductory lesson
How do you learn English?

Page 2. A letter from the people who wrote this book.
Listen to the letter.

READER: Dear students:
We hope that you learn a lot of English. We also hope that you enjoy learning it.
Do you ever think about how you learn? What things do you do to learn English? What techniques help you learn?

There are many different ways to try to learn. These are called strategies. This book will teach you many different strategies. Think about how you learn best. Try to find the strategies that work best for you.

One strategy is **clarification**. When you ask for clarification, you are "trying to understand." For example, if you don't understand something, you can say, "Could you repeat that?"

Another strategy is **prediction**. Prediction is when you think about what will happen. You guess what you will hear.

In Listening Task 1, you will learn to ask for clarification. But first, try a prediction activity.
Work with a partner.
Look at Listening Task 1 on page 3.
You already know a lot of English.
What do you think the sentences will be?
Say the sentences.
Good luck with learning English. You can do it!
Sincerely,
Marc Helgesen
Steven Brown

Page 3, Listening Task 1: What do you say when ... ?
In English, when you don't understand something, you should ask.

There are many ways to ask for **clarification**. Look at the questions. What do you think the sentences will be? Write them. [*pause*] Now listen. Were you right? Correct the sentences.

NUMBER 1
MAN: What do you say when you want someone to say something again?
WOMAN: Could you repeat that? Could you repeat that?
Excuse me? Excuse me?
Pardon? Pardon?

NUMBER 2
MAN: What do you say when you want to know how to spell a word?
WOMAN: How do you spell that? How do you spell that?

NUMBER 3

MAN: What do you say when you want to know a
word in English?
WOMAN: How do you say that in English? How do
you say that in English?

NUMBER 4

MAN: What do you say when you don't understand
something?
WOMAN: I don't understand. I don't understand.

NUMBER 5

MAN: What do you say when you understand the
meaning but don't know the answer?
WOMAN: I don't know. I don't know.

NUMBER 6

MAN: What do you say when you want the teacher
to play the tape again?
WOMAN: Once more, please. Once more, please.

Page 4, Listening Task 2: What are you listening for?

There are many ways to listen. We listen differently
for different reasons.
   Part 1. Sometimes, you have to understand only
the topic or situation.

EXAMPLE 1: The topic

Listen to the conversation. What is the most
important idea? Check your answer.

MAN: Let's go outside. We could go for a walk. Or
maybe we could play tennis.
WOMAN: Look out the window. It's raining.
MAN: Raining! Oh no.

EXAMPLE 2: Shopping

Listen. Some people are in a clothing store. What
kind of clothes are they talking about? Check your
answer.

CLERK: May I help you?
CUSTOMER: Uh, I'm looking for something for my
husband. A birthday present.
CLERK: How about a sweater?
CUSTOMER: A sweater. That's a good idea.
CLERK: We're having a sale on sweaters right now.
They're really warm.
CUSTOMER: Hmm.
CLERK: 100 percent wool.
CUSTOMER: They do look warm.
CLERK: And winter's coming.

This is called **listening for gist**. You don't need to
understand everything. You just want the general
meaning.
   Part 2. Often, you have to understand specific
information.

EXAMPLE 1: The weather

Listen. What is the weather like? Check your answer.

MAN: Let's go outside. We could go for a walk. Or
maybe we could play tennis.
WOMAN: Look out the window. It's raining.
MAN: Raining! Oh no.

EXAMPLE 2: Shopping

Look at the pictures of clothing on page 4. Listen.
How much do the sweaters cost? Write the prices
below the pictures.

CUSTOMER: How much are they?
CLERK: Let's see. The white one is thirty-five dollars.
CUSTOMER: Thirty-five?
CLERK: That's right. Thirty-five dollars. The other
one is … I think it's thirty-seven. Let me check.
That's right. The gray one is thirty-seven dollars.
CUSTOMER: Thirty-five dollars and thirty-seven
dollars. Hmm.

This is called **listening for specific information**.
Think about what information you need. Ask
yourself, "What am I listening for?"
   Part 3. Sometimes, the speaker doesn't say the
exact words, but you can still understand the
meaning.

EXAMPLE 1: The weather

Listen. Will they go outside? Check your answer.

MAN: Let's go outside. We could go for a walk. Or
maybe we could play tennis.
WOMAN: Look out the window. It's raining.
MAN: Raining! Oh no.

EXAMPLE 2: Shopping

Look at the pictures of clothing on page 4. Listen.
Which sweater does the woman buy? Circle the one
she buys.

CUSTOMER: Well, they're both nice. Gee, I'm not
sure about this one. It might be hard to keep
clean. You know things like this. They get dirty so
easily. They show spots, dirt, everything.
CLERK: Well, that one won't show dirt at all. It'll be
easy to keep clean.
CUSTOMER: I hate to say it, but Jack – my husband
– isn't very good at keeping things clean. Maybe
I'd better go for that one. It'll be easier to take
care of.
CLERK: He's going to love it. It will be easy to keep
clean.

This is called **understanding inferences**. You can
understand the meaning even though no one says
the exact words.

Unit 1 Getting to know you

Page 7, Listening Task 1: How about you?

Listen. Write answers about yourself.

NUMBER 1

MAN: What country would you like to visit? Write it in the circle.
If you could go anywhere in the world, where would you go? Write the country in the circle.

NUMBER 2

WOMAN: Write a friend's name in the triangle. What's the name of one of your friends? Write the name in the triangle.

NUMBER 3

MAN: Where are you from? Write the name of the place in the square.
In the square, write the name of your hometown.

NUMBER 4

WOMAN: What do you like to do in your free time? Write it in the triangle.
What are you interested in? Write a free-time activity in the triangle.

NUMBER 5

MAN: What don't you enjoy doing? Write it in the circle.
In the circle, write down something you don't like to do.

NUMBER 6

WOMAN: At school, what is or was your favorite subject? Write it in the square.
What class at school do you or did you like the most? Write the name of the subject in the square.

NUMBER 7

MAN: Write your favorite kind of music in the triangle.
What kind of music do you like the best? Write it in the triangle.

NUMBER 8

WOMAN: In the circle, write something you like. It can be a food, a sport, or anything else.
Write the name of something you like in the circle.

Page 8, Listening Task 2: Friends or strangers?

Listen. Are these people friends or strangers? Write "F" for "friends" and "S" for "strangers."

NUMBER 1

MAN: Hey, Ruth. How was your vacation? You look great.
RUTH: Oh, thanks. My vacation was wonderful. I had a really good time.

MAN: What did you do?
RUTH: I played a lot of tennis, caught up on my reading, and went to the beach every morning. Just took it easy.
MAN: Well it looks like you got a great tan. Welcome back.
RUTH: Thanks. But look at all this work!

NUMBER 2

[*Sound of an airplane engine*]
FIRST MAN: Wow, this is unusual. The plane's actually taking off on time! It doesn't seem to happen very often.
SECOND MAN: What? Oh, yeah, I guess so.
FIRST MAN: Do you take this flight often?
SECOND MAN: Uh, maybe three times a year, at the most.
FIRST MAN: I do a lot of business in Toronto, so I'm on this flight twice a month.
SECOND MAN: Really?
FIRST MAN: Yeah. I work for Tech-Co and I do a lot of business up there, so I …

NUMBER 3

[*Sound of street traffic, passersby*]
CHERYL: Diane!
DIANE: Cheryl! I thought you were living in Los Angeles.
CHERYL: I was, but I've moved back. I just couldn't take the big city.
DIANE: So, what are you doing now?
CHERYL: Well, I'm back in school. I'm going to become a teacher.
DIANE: Really? That sounds great. I always thought you'd be a good teacher.
CHERYL: I hope so. Listen, do you have time for coffee? We can talk about the old days.
DIANE: Sure. Let's go to Jake's.
CHERYL: That sounds good.

NUMBER 4

CLERK: Good morning. Can I help you?
CUSTOMER: Yeah, I bought a sweater last week but, uh, I don't really like the color. It looked OK here, but when I got home it looked different. Anyway, the color looked terrible. I want to return it.
CLERK: Yes, sir. Do you have the sales slip?
CUSTOMER: Uh, yeah. Here it is.
CLERK: OK. Uh-oh. Uh, sir. This was on sale when you bought it. I'm sorry, but sale items can't be returned.
CUSTOMER: What!
CLERK: I'm sorry, but that's the store policy. Things on sale can't be returned.
CUSTOMER: That's crazy. Let me talk to the manager.
CLERK: Just a minute, please. [*picks up phone; dials*] Ms. Wilson, there a gentleman here who'd like to return a sale item …

NUMBER 5

[*Party sounds*]

JACK: Oh, excuse me. It's pretty crowded in here.

LUIS: Yeah, and it's getting hot. Nice party though.

JACK: Yeah, Kate knows how to throw 'em. Oh, I'm Jack Michaels.

LUIS: Luis Santos. Nice to meet you, Jack.

JACK: Good to meet you. How do you know Kate?

LUIS: Oh, we went to the same university. And you?

JACK: Well, we work together.

LUIS: Yeah? How do you like working for Newton?

JACK: Oh, it's OK. I have a pretty interesting job …

NUMBER 6

[*Sound of street traffic*]

FIRST WOMAN: Excuse me – I wonder if you could tell me if there's a bank near here.

SECOND WOMAN: Mmm. Let's see. Yeah, Central Bank is pretty close. It's just a few blocks down this street. Just go straight and it'll be on your left.

FIRST WOMAN: Just down this street?

SECOND WOMAN: You can't miss it. It's on the corner.

FIRST WOMAN: Great, thanks.

SECOND WOMAN: Not at all.

Unit 2 What's your number?

Page 10, Listening Task 1: May I ask your number?

Listen. Find the correct form for each conversation. Write the missing numbers in the correct places.

NUMBER 1

[*Telephone rings*]

PAULA: I'm not here. I don't want to talk to anybody.

ROOMMATE: Oh, Paula.

PAULA: Just take a message. I'll be upstairs.

ROOMMATE: All right. [*picks up phone*] Hello.

JIM: Hi. Is Paula there?

ROOMMATE: Sorry, she's at school. Can I take a message?

JIM: Yeah. This is Jim Robbins. Could you ask her to call me at work?

ROOMMATE: Sure. Does Paula know your number?

JIM: I'm not sure. But the number is 555-2137.

ROOMMATE: 555-2137. OK. I'll tell her to call you.

JIM: Thanks. Goodbye.

ROOMMATE: Goodbye. [*hangs up phone*] Paula, it was Jim Robbins.

PAULA: Jim? I wanted to talk to him!

ROOMMATE: Uhh!

NUMBER 2

CLERK: May I help you?

STUDENT: I'd like two tickets for the Student Association Concert.

CLERK: OK, you're a student here, right?

STUDENT: That's right.

CLERK: Do you have your ID, uh, your student identification card? I need the number.

STUDENT: Yeah. Here it is. The number's 94-10538.

CLERK: 94-10538. OK. Thanks. Here are your tickets.

STUDENT: Thank you.

NUMBER 3

[*Caller dials phone; phone rings; pick up*]

OPERATOR: Good evening, Hit Parade Order Service.

CALLER: Hello. I want to order the *Awesome Hits of the '90s* CD. I saw it on a television commercial last night.

OPERATOR: *Awesome Hits of the '90s* CD. OK. What's your name?

CALLER: Tom Davis. That's D-A-V-I-S.

OPERATOR: Tom Davis. OK, do you want to charge it on Vista, Mastercharge, or American Expense?

CALLER: Vista.

OPERATOR: What's your credit card number, please?

CALLER: It's 34862 212039 62008.

OPERATOR: 34862 212039 62008?

CALLER: Right.

OPERATOR: And what's the expiration date of your card?

CALLER: Let's see. March …

NUMBER 4

MAN: Could you help me out for a minute? I want to mail a package and I need help with the address label.

WOMAN: Sure. Let's see, you're sending this to Eri Sato?

MAN: Yes.

WOMAN: What's her address?

MAN: 3209 West 145th Street in Los Angeles.

WOMAN: 3209 West 145th. Do you know the ZIP code?

MAN: Uh. ZIP code? You mean like the postal code?

WOMAN: That's right. What's the postal code?

MAN: Let me see … Here it is: 90025.

WOMAN: 90025. OK, I'll drop it by the post office.

MAN: Thanks. Hmm. ZIP code.

Page 11, Listening Task 2: Fast math

Listen. Write the numbers. How fast can you figure out the answers? Try to write the answers before you hear them.

T4

NUMBER 1

WOMAN: How much is three hundred eighty-nine plus fifty-six? [*pause*] How much is three hundred eighty-nine plus fifty-six? [*musical scale*] The answer? Four hundred forty-five. Four forty-five.

NUMBER 2

WOMAN: How much is one thousand eight hundred seventy-seven plus three thousand four hundred sixty? [*pause*] How much is one thousand eight hundred seventy-seven plus three thousand four hundred sixty? [*musical scale*] The answer? Five thousand three hundred thirty-seven. Five thousand three hundred and thirty-seven.

NUMBER 3

WOMAN: How much is four thousand eight hundred fifty-two plus two thousand nine hundred eleven? [*pause*] How much is four thousand eight hundred fifty-two plus two thousand nine hundred eleven? [*musical scale*] The answer? Seven thousand seven hundred sixty-three. Seven thousand seven hundred and sixty-three.

NUMBER 4

WOMAN: How much is one hundred twenty-eight times three? [*pause*] How much is one hundred twenty-eight times three? [*musical scale*] The answer? Three hundred eighty-four. Three hundred and eighty-four.

NUMBER 5

WOMAN: How much is seven hundred forty-six times five? [*pause*] How much is seven hundred forty-six times five? [*musical scale*] The answer? Three thousand seven hundred thirty. Three thousand seven hundred and thirty.

NUMBER 6

WOMAN: How much is one thousand eight hundred fifty-seven times seven? [*pause*] How much is one thousand eight hundred fifty-seven times seven? [*musical scale*] The answer? Twelve thousand nine hundred ninety-nine. Twelve thousand nine hundred and ninety-nine.

Now listen to two conversations in a department store. Figure out the totals before you hear them. Write the prices.

NUMBER 7

CUSTOMER: How much are these CDs?

CLERK: They're nineteen ninety-five each.

CUSTOMER: Nineteen ninety-five? OK. I'll take these three.

CLERK: OK. Three CDs at nineteen ninety-five. [*musical scale*] That comes to fifty-nine dollars and eighty-five cents.

CUSTOMER: Fifty-nine eighty-five. Can I write a check?

NUMBER 8

FIRST CLERK: May I help you?

CUSTOMER: Yeah, I'd like these.

FIRST CLERK: OK. One sweater. Thirty-five fifty …

SECOND CLERK: [*punches in price on cash register*] Sweater, thirty-five fifty.

FIRST CLERK: And a shirt. Twenty-three seventy-seven.

SECOND CLERK: Shirt, twenty-three seventy-seven. [*musical scale*]

FIRST CLERK: The total is fifty-nine dollars and twenty-seven cents.

CUSTOMER: Fifty-nine twenty-seven? OK.

Unit 3 I'm hungry!

Page 13, Listening Task 1: Now that's a sandwich!

Listen. What ingredients go in this sandwich? Write or draw them.

FIRST MAN: Uh, what are you doing?

SECOND MAN: Making some sandwiches for the picnic. I love a good sandwich, but have you noticed how hard it is to get a really good one around here?

FIRST MAN: What do you mean? They sell sandwiches all over.

SECOND MAN: Yeah, but they're not very good. I mean, for a real sandwich, the ingredients – the meat, the cheese, and stuff – should be at least as thick as the bread.

FIRST MAN: Yeah, well, I can see that. But what are you putting in them?

SECOND MAN: Well, I like to start with roast beef. You put a few slices of roast beef on bread.

FIRST MAN: You've got a lot of beef there.

SECOND MAN: Yeah, you need lots of roast beef at the bottom. Maybe five or six slices. Think of it as the base. It needs to be solid. Then, let's see. How about turkey? Yeah, a few pieces of turkey.

FIRST MAN: Roast beef, then turkey. You think you have enough meat? How about some vegetables on that?

SECOND MAN: Yeah, um, how about some sliced onions? On top of the meat we'll put sliced onions and then, hmm, some tomatoes and mushrooms.

FIRST MAN: Onions, tomatoes, mushrooms. OK. That looks good. Maybe a few more mushrooms.

SECOND MAN: Yeah, a few more mushrooms. Hmm, looks great. And on top of that, a layer of cheese.

FIRST MAN: Yeah. Let's put some lettuce on that cheese.

SECOND MAN: Right. Cheese, then lettuce. Uh, do you like mustard?

FIRST MAN: Mustard? Yeah.

SECOND MAN: OK. Let's put on some mustard. And now the other piece of bread.

FIRST MAN: Wow. It looks great.

SECOND MAN: Now *these* are sandwiches.

FIRST MAN: Sandwiches? Actually, they look more like mountains.

SECOND MAN: Yeah. Let's eat them now. Why wait for the picnic?

Page 14, Listening Task 2: What's cooking?

Listen. Some students are learning how to make jambalaya, a dish from the southern part of the United States. Put the pictures in order.

TEACHER: Good evening, everyone.

ALL STUDENTS: Good evening. Hi.

TEACHER: Last class we learned how to make New England clam chowder. Well, this time we're going to learn how to cook a dish from the southern part of the United States. Has anyone heard of jambalaya?

FIRST STUDENT: It's a kind of seafood dish, isn't it?

SECOND STUDENT: Yeah, I ate it when I was in New Orleans last year. It was pretty spicy.

TEACHER: Did you like it?

SECOND STUDENT: Yeah, it was good. I'd like to learn to make it.

TEACHER: Well, that's what we're going to make tonight. Jambalaya is from Louisiana. It's called "Cajun" food. And I think you'll find it's easy to make. It has a lot of ingredients, but they're all necessary for a good jambalaya. So here we go. Let's see, the first thing we have to do is fry the meat. [*sound of meat sizzling*] Now, while the meat is frying, I'll chop up the vegetables. We need to chop up an onion, some celery, a green pepper, and some garlic. [*sound of vegetables being chopped*] OK. Next we want to add the vegetables to the meat and fry them – sauté them, actually – in butter for about five minutes. [*sound of meat and vegetables sizzling*] Are there any questions while the vegetables are frying?

FIRST STUDENT: You just fry the vegetables and meat together?

TEACHER: That's right. In the meantime, I'll cut up the tomatoes. Now we add them to the frying pan. Tomatoes don't need much cooking. Hmm … it's looking tasty. Now let's see. Next we have to stir in all those spices. Spices are the heart of the jambalaya. There's chili powder, three different kinds of pepper, and Tabasco sauce.

THIRD STUDENT: What kinds of pepper?

TEACHER: Oh, white pepper, black pepper, and cayenne pepper. That makes it hot and spicy. Now, while the spices are cooking, I'll peel the shrimp. Everyone has peeled shrimp before, right?

STUDENTS: Yeah.

TEACHER: Oh good. OK. Now we put everything together in this large pot: the meat and vegetables, the shrimp, and two cups of chicken broth. [*sound of ingredients going into the pot*] Then give it a stir. Make sure you stir it really thoroughly, especially with all the spices and everything. OK, that's about it. Now we just cook the mixture.

THIRD STUDENT: How long?

TEACHER: Well, once it starts to boil, we stir in the rice. Then we lower the heat, put a cover on the pot, and just let it cook for about 35 minutes. While we're letting it cook, let's take a look at some of the foods that you can serve with jambalaya …

Unit 4 Gestures

Page 16, Listening Task 1: What does that mean?

One person in each conversation above uses a gesture. The first speaker is on the left. Listen. What do the gestures mean in these places? Check the correct meaning.

NUMBER 1: What does a nod mean in most countries?

MAN: So do you want to do that?

WOMAN: Yes, that sounds great.

MAN: So your answer is yes? Good.

NUMBER 2: What do raised eyebrows mean in Tonga?

MAN: I'm happy to tell you that I agree. I'm going to say yes. I think it's a good decision … a good idea.

WOMAN: Wonderful!

NUMBER 3: What does tapping your head mean in Argentina?

FIRST WOMAN: Well, have you decided yet?

SECOND WOMAN: Just a minute. I need a little time to think about this. Can I let you know later, after I decide?

FIRST WOMAN: Sure, take your time. Give it some thought.

NUMBER 4: What does tapping your elbow mean in the Netherlands?

WOMAN: Who are we going to give the job to? How about Mr. Van Horn?

T6

MAN: Mr. Van Horn? Ah, I'm not sure. He's a nice person, of course, but I don't know if we can depend on him. I'm not sure he'll get the job done.

NUMBER 5: What does circling your head mean in most parts of Europe?
WOMAN: The guy is crazy. I mean, I don't understand him at all. He is weird. I mean …
MAN: Come on. Calm down. He can't be that strange.

NUMBER 6: What does flicking your chin mean in Italy?
FIRST MAN: And I just know you'll find our products to be absolutely the best. The prices are low and the quality is just what you need.
SECOND MAN: No, thank you. Thank you for your time.
FIRST MAN: Now, I'd suggest that you think about the new model. It's a bit more expensive than the old one. But you'll find …
SECOND MAN: Look, today is not the day to talk about it. I'm very busy. I don't want to be rude but I must ask you to leave. You have to leave now.
FIRST MAN: Well, maybe a different day. [*door opens and closes*]
SECOND MAN: [*groans*]

NUMBER 7: What does thumbs up mean in the United States?
FIRST WOMAN: So, good news I hope?
SECOND WOMAN: Great. Everything is just fine. Things are looking good.
FIRST WOMAN: Wonderful.

NUMBER 8: What does tossing your head mean in Germany?
WOMAN: Peter!
PETER: Yeah?
WOMAN: Peter?
PETER: Just a minute. I'll be right there. [*footsteps*] Yes, what is it?
WOMAN: The reason I asked you to come over here is because I want to show you …

Page 17, Listening Task 2: It's different there.
Listen. In some places, the gestures have a different meaning. Write the names of the countries next to the meanings.

NUMBER 1
WOMAN: You know, a "nod" – moving your head up and down – means "yes" in most places, but not everywhere. Did you know that in Greece a nod means "no"?
MAN: It means "no" in Greece? I'm surprised.

NUMBER 2
MAN: I didn't know "raised eyebrows" means "yes" in Tonga. It means something very different in Peru.
WOMAN: Yeah? What does it mean there?
MAN: Money. Raised eyebrows is a gesture for money in Peru.
WOMAN: Hmm.

NUMBER 3
WOMAN: Um, Alberto, you said that tapping your head means "I'm thinking" in Argentina.
MAN: That's right.
WOMAN: You'd better be careful about using that gesture here in Canada. It means someone is crazy.
MAN: Oh, it means "crazy" in Canada? I didn't know that. I'll be careful.

NUMBER 4
MAN: You know, it's interesting that in the Netherlands, tapping your elbow means you can't depend on someone. In Colombia, they use the same gesture, but it has a different meaning.
WOMAN: What does it mean in Colombia?
MAN: Well, it means someone is cheap. That person doesn't like to spend money.
WOMAN: Oh.

NUMBER 5
WOMAN: Here's an interesting one. You know how "circling your head" means that a person's crazy?
MAN: Yeah.
WOMAN: Guess what it means in the Netherlands.
MAN: The Netherlands? I have no idea.
WOMAN: It means someone is calling on the telephone. You know, like dialing a phone.
MAN: That's interesting.

NUMBER 6
MAN: So flicking your chin means "go away" in Italy, right?
WOMAN: Yes.
MAN: Guess what it means in Brazil.
WOMAN: In Brazil? I don't know.
MAN: That's right.
WOMAN: Huh?
MAN: In Brazil, flicking your chin means "I don't know."
WOMAN: "I don't know" is the meaning?
MAN: Right.

NUMBER 7
WOMAN: Well, everything is "thumbs up" for my trip to Nigeria. I've never been to Africa before. I'm really looking forward to it.
MAN: Ah, you'd better be careful with that expression in Nigeria.
WOMAN: Huh?

MAN: Thumbs up. In Nigeria, it means … um … well, it has a very bad meaning. Don't use that gesture. It will get you into a lot of trouble.
WOMAN: Oh, thanks for telling me.

NUMBER 8
MAN: You said tossing your head means "come here" for Germans?
WOMAN: That's right. But there are some other meanings. In India, it means "yes." But it has the opposite meaning in Italy. In Italy it means "no."
MAN: Hmm, "yes" in India, "no" in Italy. Isn't it interesting how the same thing can have such different meanings?
WOMAN: It sure is.

Unit 5 Didn't you see that sign?

Page 19, Listening Task 1: What do they really mean?
What do you think these signs mean? Check the correct box. [*pause*] Now listen. What do the signs mean? Circle the answers.

NUMBER 1
[*Sound of street traffic*]
FIRST TOURIST: Say, that building looks interesting.
SECOND TOURIST: Yeah, let's go in and see.
GUARD: Hey, you two! Where do you think you're going?
SECOND TOURIST: Ah, well, we just wanted to see …
GUARD: You wanted to see? You wanted to see? Well, didn't you see that sign?
FIRST TOURIST: The sign?
GUARD: Yeah, right there. You can't go in there.
FIRST TOURIST: Oh, ah, gee. We're sorry. We didn't know.
GUARD: Yeah, well now you do.

NUMBER 2
MAN: So the office is, what, on the fifth floor?
WOMAN: That's right, fifth floor. Room 503.
MAN: Where's the – oh, there it is. Well, shall we go up?
WOMAN: Yeah. Let's go.

NUMBER 3
[*Sound of car engine*]
FIRST MAN: I'm getting tired of driving. Let's take a break.
SECOND MAN: That sounds good. Hey, look. There's something interesting right here.

FIRST MAN: Yeah, what?
SECOND MAN: I don't know, but there's a sign. You know, for a park or a museum or something. Let's check it out.
FIRST MAN: OK.

NUMBER 4
[*Sound of airport terminal*]
MAN: So, only twenty minutes late. Not bad for this airport.
WOMAN: Yeah, really. Shall we take the airport bus or do you want to catch a taxi?
MAN: Look, we're going to be here for a few days. Why don't we just rent a car?
WOMAN: Yeah, that would be better than trying to catch cabs all the time.
MAN: Oh, look. There's a place over there.

NUMBER 5
[*Sound of hiking in woods*]
FIRST WOMAN: It sure is beautiful out here.
SECOND WOMAN: Yeah. Hmm, look at that sign over there. Let's go see.
FIRST WOMAN: OK. [*footsteps*] Wow! Look at those trees! They're incredible.
SECOND WOMAN: I've never seen anything like that! That's great.
FIRST WOMAN: Yeah.

NUMBER 6
[*Sound of car engine*]
WIFE: Oh, look, Gene. There's another point of interest. I just love these old places.
HUSBAND: Another one? Do we have to stop?
WIFE: Of course. Let's see. [*sound of page turning*] It says in this guidebook it's over two hundred years old! You know, I didn't realize there were so many places like this in Canada.
HUSBAND: All we've done for two days is visit old buildings. Can't we find a historic swimming pool or restaurant or movie theater or something?
WIFE: Well, I guess we could try …

NUMBER 7
LIFEGUARD: Attention swimmers by the rocks. Please be careful. The water is very deep over there. Please be careful. Swim with a partner. – These kids drive me crazy sometimes.

NUMBER 8
MAN: So, when are the others going to get here?
WOMAN: It's what – ten-thirty? They're supposed to be here by now. I told everyone to meet here by ten-fifteen.
MAN: Oh, here they come now. Hey, guys!

Page 20, Listening Task 2: You can't do that.

Rangers work in parks and campgrounds. They take care of the park and make sure people are safe. Listen. A ranger is explaining the park rules. Some things in the picture are against the rules. Cross out the activities that are against the rules.

[*Sound of rustling leaves, birds, crickets*]

RANGER: Good evening. I'd like to welcome you all to the Red River State Park. I'm Ranger Johnson and in just a few minutes Ranger Green will talk to you about some of the different kinds of animals that live here in the park. But before that, I'd like to go over a few of the rules for those of you who are here for the first time. Please remember that we do want you to enjoy your stay. These rules are for your protection.

First of all, you cannot have an open fire at your campsite.

FIRST CAMPER: No fires?

RANGER: No *open* fires. It's fine to have a campfire, but you need to use the firepits. Every campsite has a fire area that is surrounded with rocks. Build your fires there. And don't cut your own firewood. We sell firewood at the camp shop, so please, buy it there and don't cut your own. We have a lot of visitors in the park and have to be very careful about cutting trees.

Also you shouldn't leave food out. Don't leave it on the picnic tables, for example. It's best to keep your food locked in the trunk of your car. We have a lot of animals in the park who would love to take your food.

SECOND CAMPER: Animals? What kind of animals? Bears?

RANGER: No, mostly smaller animals like raccoons, possums, or squirrels. The bears are in the northern part of the park and usually don't come near the campsites. But you should be careful. There are a lot of beautiful hiking trails in the park. When you go hiking, always go with another person. It's easy to get lost. Let me emphasize that. You really have to go with a partner. It's a new rule. We had some problems last year.

The other thing is the swimming area. Children cannot swim alone. They must be with a parent or other adult.

THIRD CAMPER: Awww. My parents!

RANGER: No, it's important. You have to be with a grown-up.

So, those are the basic rules. Any questions about them? I do hope you enjoy your stay here. Now, I'd like to introduce Ranger Green who will tell us about …

Unit 6 How do you feel?

Page 22, Listening Task 1: I really should be more careful.

Listen. Two friends are talking about health. Do they do these things? Write "yes" or "no."

[*Sound of newspaper being folded*]

ANDY: Hey, June, there's a new quiz in the paper. I love to fill these things out.

JUNE: Yeah, they're always fun. What's this one about?

ANDY: It's about health.

JUNE: OK, read it to me. I'll keep score.

ANDY: OK. Number one. Do you smoke more than ten cigarettes a day?

JUNE: That's easy. I gave up smoking three years ago.

ANDY: Right. You know, I should too.

JUNE: Yeah. I've heard that before.

ANDY: No. No, really. I'm going to. But for now, I'd have to say "yes." OK, number two. Do you have a checkup at your doctor's office at least once a year?

JUNE: Yeah. The company makes us go to the doctor every year. How about you?

ANDY: Well, I went to the doctor, let's see … about three years ago.

JUNE: You should go more often.

ANDY: Yeah. OK, here's a big "no" for me. Number three. Do you sleep more than ten hours a night? I sleep eight hours every night.

JUNE: Me too. We're both OK there. Neither of us sleeps too much.

ANDY: Great. I don't have to read number four then. They want to know if you sleep less than five hours.

JUNE: No problem there.

ANDY: OK. Number five. Do you exercise for twenty minutes at least three times a week?

JUNE: Exercise? What kind?

ANDY: They say cycling, walking, swimming, dancing, etc.

JUNE: Well, no. I mean, I ride my bike sometimes. I go dancing every once in a while. But no, I really don't get much exercise.

ANDY: Yeah, I should get more exercise too. OK, number six. Do you live in a city?

JUNE: Well, we're both in trouble there.

ANDY: Yeah, this is a big city. All the noise, all the stress.

JUNE: Yeah, it would be better to move to a smaller town. Lots of trees …

ANDY: Where are you going to find a job?

JUNE: Hmm … you have a point. So, there's a "yes" for both of us.

ANDY: Number 7. Do you work more than ten hours a day?

JUNE: No. But you've been working a lot lately.

ANDY: I'm really tired. I should work a lot less. But we've been busy, though.

JUNE: You really should slow down.

ANDY: It's not that easy. Last question. Is your life very stressful?

JUNE: Stressful? Yeah, I guess I'd have to say "yes." I should relax more.

ANDY: I definitely should relax more. You know what? It's surprising I'm not dead already.

Page 23, Listening Task 2: Stressed out

Listen. Mia is feeling a lot of stress. Which things does her friend suggest? Check them. What does she say about each idea? Write one thing.

FRIEND: Are you OK, Mia? You look beat. You look really tired.

MIA: I am. I can't seem to sleep at night. I've been under a lot of pressure lately – a lot of stress.

FRIEND: What's up?

MIA: I've got a million things to do. I'm busy at work. I'm working on the house too, you know. I'm trying to fix it up. I need to finish it before winter. Just lots of deadlines.

FRIEND: Any way I can help?

MIA: Thanks, but not really. It's just things I have to do.

FRIEND: Well, you need to manage that stress a little better. Are you getting any exercise?

MIA: Who has time?

FRIEND: You really should ride a bicycle to the store, or walk to work a couple days a week, or go swimming at the community center. It helps me to get exercise when I'm busy. You don't have to become a fitness nut, you know.

MIA: That is a good suggestion. It's just the time, you know. I'm always thinking of what I should be doing.

FRIEND: No wonder you can't sleep. A lot of people learn to meditate or learn yoga. Meditation and yoga are supposed to be good ways to deal with stress. They help you relax.

MIA: Yoga? Maybe I'll call the community center. They might have some classes there.

FRIEND: You know, another thing you can do is take vitamins. You use up a lot of vitamins and you don't get them in your meals all the time. They won't help the stress, but they might help your body handle it better. You really should take vitamins every day.

MIA: Yeah, I should get some. Thanks.

FRIEND: How about going out with Rosa and me this Friday? It'll do you good. We could see a movie, make you forget your problems. Have a little fun.

MIA: You know, you're right about all of this. Let's go somewhere Friday night, have dinner, see a movie. That'll be fun.

FRIEND: Now you're talking!

MIA: OK. See you Friday. Got to get back to work!

FRIEND: Mia, you're hopeless, truly hopeless.

Unit 7 Where is it?

Page 25, Listening Task 1: The park

Listen. Where are these places? Write the numbers on the map.

NUMBER 1: The playground

[*Sound of park: birds chirping, music*]

MAN: Excuse me. Is there a playground in the park?

WOMAN: Oh, what a cute little boy. Is he your son?

MAN: Yeah.

WOMAN: Umm, the playground. It's to your right as soon as you go through the entrance. You'll see some trees in back of it.

MAN: To the right, just inside the entrance.

WOMAN: Yeah. There are a lot of swings and a big slide. Oh your son will love it.

MAN: Thanks.

NUMBER 2: The boat rental

FIRST MAN: I've never been here before. Can you rent boats and take them out on the lake?

SECOND MAN: Oh, sure. There's a boat rental near the statue.

FIRST MAN: Near the statue?

SECOND MAN: Yeah. See it right by the lake next to the trees?

FIRST MAN: Oh, yeah. There are the boats.

NUMBER 3: A telephone booth

WOMAN: Excuse me. Is there a telephone around here?

MAN: Oh yeah. It's just past the tennis courts.

WOMAN: I don't understand. Just past the tennis courts?

MAN: Yeah. Turn right after the tennis courts. It's near the wall, the back wall of the zoo.

WOMAN: Thank you.

NUMBER 4: The hot dog stand

FIRST WOMAN: I'm hungry. Would you like to get something to eat?

SECOND WOMAN: Yeah, I'm hungry too. Do you know if there's a restaurant near here?

FIRST WOMAN: Well, it's not a restaurant, but I saw a hot dog stand near the front gate.

SECOND WOMAN: Near the entrance? I don't remember seeing one.

T10

FIRST WOMAN: It was to the left of the entrance as we walked in.
SECOND WOMAN: Really? Hot dogs are fine. Let's go there. [*footsteps*]

NUMBER 5: *The beach*
MAN: Excuse me, where's the beach?
WOMAN: Oh, it's on the opposite side of the lake.
MAN: The other side?
WOMAN: Yes. It's between the lake and the trees at the back of the park.
MAN: Oh I see. Thank you.

NUMBER 6: *The zoo entrance*
[*Sound of children playing*]
WOMAN: Excuse me. Do you know if the zoo entrance is inside the park?
MAN: Yes, it is. It's all the way in the back, past the tennis courts.
WOMAN: Past the tennis courts?
MAN: Yes. Follow the path to the very end and turn right after the trees. Keep going and you'll come to the zoo entrance.
WOMAN: Thank you.

Page 26, Listening Task 2: How do I get there?
The Hotel Lotte is in Seoul, Korea. It is a large and busy hotel. Listen. Some guests are at the front desk. They are asking for directions to these five places. Follow the directions. Write the numbers on the map.

NUMBER 1
[*Sound of busy hotel lobby*]
CLERK: May I help you, ma'am?
WOMAN: Yes, I have an appointment at the Bank of Korea. Where is that?
CLERK: It's fairly near here actually. Turn right when you get outside the hotel, then right again at the corner. Walk straight two blocks till you get to an intersection. It's on the right, on the corner.
WOMAN: Let me see if I've got that. Right outside the hotel, right at the corner, and straight two blocks?
CLERK: That's right, ma'am. They are rather long blocks.
WOMAN: I see. Thank you.

NUMBER 2
CLERK: May I help you.
MAN: I understand there's a good map store near here.
CLERK: Oh, you must mean the Jung-an Map Shop. Yes, they have an excellent selection. Uh, turn right when you leave the hotel. At the first corner, turn left. Then walk about three and a half blocks. It'll be on your left.
MAN: Right as I leave the hotel. Then left and walk three and a half blocks. Thanks.

NUMBER 3
MAN: I need to go to the British Embassy. Is it near here?
CLERK: Very close, sir. Go out of the hotel and turn left. Go straight toward the palace. There's a big park at the end of the street.
MAN: Left, then straight to the park.
CLERK: That's right. Cross the street. Uh, there's an underpass. Go under the big street. Turn right at the palace.
MAN: Right at the palace?
CLERK: Yes, the British Embassy is just past the palace. You'll pass City Hall on your right. Make the first left after the park. You'll see the British Embassy on your right.
MAN: The first left past the park.
CLERK: Yes. If you get to the Koreana Hotel, you've gone too far.
MAN: Thank you.

NUMBER 4
WOMAN: Excuse me, could you tell me how to get to the National Museum?
CLERK: It's rather far. You can catch a taxi in front of the hotel.
WOMAN: The weather is so nice. Is it possible to walk?
CLERK: It's probably a twenty-five or thirty minute walk.
WOMAN: That sounds perfect. How do I get there?
CLERK: When you leave the hotel, turn left and go straight. Cross that big street. Uh, use the underpass. You'll see a park. At the park, turn right, just past City Hall.
WOMAN: City Hall. OK, I saw that yesterday.
CLERK: Then you go straight, along that big street, for about, oh, twenty or thirty minutes. That street ends where it meets another large street.
WOMAN: Let's see. I'd be going … north?
CLERK: Yes, ma'am. Go past the U.S. Embassy. That's on your right. You'll come to a T-junction. The museum is right there at the end of the street.
WOMAN: At the T-junction?
CLERK: Yes. Just cross the street – go under the street. When you come up, it will be right there. It's easy to find.
WOMAN: OK, thank you very much.
CLERK: You're welcome.

NUMBER 5
CLERK: Good morning. How can I help you?
MAN: I'd like to go the shrines. How do I get there?
CLERK: There are many shrines in Seoul, sir. Is there a particular one?
MAN: [*sound of pages turning*] Uh. Here it is, the Chan—, Changm—. Uh, the ancestral shrines.

CLERK: The Chongmyo ancestral shrines? Yes, sir. They're quite a ways away. I'd suggest you take a taxi or the subway.

MAN: The subway? That's sounds like an adventure. Where do I catch it?

CLERK: You can get the subway at City Hall Station. Turn left when you leave the hotel. Go straight ahead. You'll see City Hall on the right. Go down one of the entrances to City Hall Station.

MAN: City Hall Station. OK.

CLERK: Right. Take the subway to Chongro sam-ka Station. "Sam" means three. Chongro sam-ka "three-ka" station. It's the second stop.

MAN: Chongro three-ka station.

CLERK: That's correct. When you leave the station, walk east. That's the same direction the train was going. You'll see a big park on your left. That's the north side of the street.

MAN: A big park, north of the subway line.

CLERK: That's right. Walk directly through the park. The shrines will be right in front of you, inside the park.

MAN: The shrines are in the park.

CLERK: I'm sure you'll be able to find them. Ah, would you like me to write you a note? You can show it to someone if you get lost.

MAN: That would be wonderful.

Unit 8 The world market

Page 28, Listening Task 1: World Trade Expo!

People are shopping at an international trade fair. Each country has a display. Listen. What countries are selling these products? Write the nationalities.

NUMBER 1

[*Sound of busy trade fair*]

CUSTOMER: I'm looking for leather goods. Shoes, bags, that sort of thing.

CLERK: Have you visited the Spanish booth? They have a wide variety of leather goods.

CUSTOMER: OK. Leather things at Spain's booth. Thanks.

NUMBER 2

CUSTOMER: Excuse me, I'm looking for cameras.

CLERK: Cameras. Well, you might try the Japanese booth. They have a lot of cameras along with their electronics goods.

CUSTOMER: OK. That sounds good.

NUMBER 3

CUSTOMER: Can you help me? I'm looking for lumber and wood products.

CLERK: You want the Canadian booth. They're displaying a lot of wood products at the Canadian booth.

CUSTOMER: Thanks.

NUMBER 4

CUSTOMER: Uh, hi. Could you help me? I heard someone has these new computers and they're really fast. Do you know where I can find them?

CLERK: Yes, the United States booth has a lot of computers. Those are probably what you're looking for.

CUSTOMER: Great!

NUMBER 5

CLERK: Can I help you?

CUSTOMER: I hope so. Where can I find watches and clocks?

CLERK: Have you tried Taiwan's booth? Taiwan has a lot of watches and clocks.

NUMBER 6

CLERK: May I help you?

CUSTOMER: Yes, I'm looking for electronics exhibits. I want to see some TVs, videos, CDs, that kind of thing.

CLERK: Well, several countries are displaying electronics. Korea's selection is very large this year.

CUSTOMER: Mmm. The Korean booth. OK.

NUMBER 7

CUSTOMER: Excuse me. I'm looking for industrial chemicals.

CLERK: Have you tried Germany's booth?

CUSTOMER: I'm sorry?

CLERK: The German booth.

CUSTOMER: Oh.

NUMBER 8

CUSTOMER: Excuse me. Is there coffee anywhere around here?

CLERK: Ah, yes, ma'am. The Brazilian booth has a very large display. Coffee is Brazil's largest export, you know.

Page 29, Listening Task 2: Where can I find that?

Listen. The shoppers in Listening Task 1 are asking directions. Write the countries in the correct places.

NUMBER 1

[*Sound of busy trade fair*]

CUSTOMER: I'm looking for leather goods. Shoes, bags, that sort of thing.

CLERK: Have you visited the Spanish booth? They have a wide variety of leather goods.

CUSTOMER: OK. Leather things at Spain's booth. Thanks. Umm, where is that?

CLERK: It's to your left, in the West Wing of the building. You'll see it across from the Netherlands display.

CUSTOMER: Across from the Netherlands display.

CLERK: Yes. It's next to the U.K., uh, the United Kingdom's booth.

NUMBER 2

CUSTOMER: Excuse me, I'm looking for cameras.

CLERK: Cameras. Well, you might try the Japanese booth. They have a lot of cameras along with their electronics goods.

CUSTOMER: OK. That sounds good. Now, where are they?

CLERK: The Japanese display is in the West Wing, to your left. The easiest way to get there is to go to the fountain and turn left. It's at the end of the West Wing.

CUSTOMER: Thank you very much.

NUMBER 3

CUSTOMER: Can you help me? I'm looking for lumber and wood products.

CLERK: You want the Canadian booth. They're displaying a lot of wood products at the Canadian booth.

CUSTOMER: Thanks. Could you tell me where that is?

CLERK: Go straight down this hall. It's at the other end of the building in the North Wing.

CUSTOMER: North Wing, straight down the hall.

CLERK: That's correct. It's at the very end. You'll pass the Indian booth on the left and the Italian booth on the right.

CUSTOMER: Pass India and Italy. All the way to the end. Got it. Thanks.

NUMBER 4

CUSTOMER: Uh, hi. Could you help me? I heard someone has these new computers and they're really fast. Do you know where I can find them?

CLERK: Yes, the United States booth has a lot of computers. Those are probably what you're looking for.

CUSTOMER: Great! Can you tell me where the U.S. booth is?

CLERK: In the East Wing. The U.S. booth is at the end of the wing. It's that big booth against the wall, just past the Swiss booth.

CUSTOMER: At the end of the East Wing, past Switzerland. Thank you!

NUMBER 5

CLERK: Can I help you?

CUSTOMER: I hope so. Where can I find watches and clocks?

CLERK: Have you tried Taiwan's booth? Taiwan has a lot of watches and clocks.

CUSTOMER: Where is the Taiwanese booth located?

CLERK: It's in the East Wing, across from Singapore, between Switzerland and Poland.

CUSTOMER: East Wing, across from Singapore?

CLERK: That's right.

NUMBER 6

CLERK: May I help you?

CUSTOMER: Yes, I'm looking for electronics exhibits. I want to see some TVs, videos, CDs, that kind of thing.

CLERK: Well, several countries are displaying electronics. Korea's selection is very large this year.

CUSTOMER: Mmm. The Korean booth. OK. And where can I find it?

CLERK: It's just around the corner to the left, in the West Wing, next to the French booth.

CUSTOMER: That's the same wing as the U.K. booth?

CLERK: That's right. Across from the U.K., between the Netherlands and France.

NUMBER 7

CUSTOMER: Excuse me. I'm looking for industrial chemicals.

CLERK: Have you tried Germany's booth?

CUSTOMER: I'm sorry?

CLERK: The German booth.

CUSTOMER: Oh. Where it is?

CLERK: It's in the East Wing, next to Singapore.

CUSTOMER: Is that across from Switzerland?

CLERK: That's right.

NUMBER 8

CUSTOMER: Excuse me. Is there coffee anywhere around here?

CLERK: Ah, yes, ma'am. The Brazilian booth has a very large display. Coffee is Brazil's largest export, you know.

CUSTOMER: Ah, no.

CLERK: Yes, it's easy to find. Go straight. It's just past the fountain, on your left.

CUSTOMER: Uh, well.

CLERK: It's right next to the Indian booth. Just before India's booth. Across from Poland.

CUSTOMER: Wait. You don't understand. I want a cup of coffee. Is there a coffee shop around here?

CLERK: A coffee shop? Oh, I see. Well, I think there's one across from …

Unit 9   What do they look like?

Page 31, Listening Task 1: They've changed a little.

Listen. Two friends are talking about these people. The people have changed since these pictures were taken. Circle what has changed.

WOMAN: So what's new with you, Tom?
TOM: Well, I met a really nice woman.
WOMAN: Yeah? That's great!
TOM: Yeah, she works with my sister. We've been going out for a couple of months now and, well, things look good.
WOMAN: So, do you have a picture of her?
TOM: Oh, I just happen to have one. [*sound of picture being taken out of a wallet*]
WOMAN: Oh great.
TOM: This picture is a year old, so she looks a little different now. We haven't taken any pictures together yet.
WOMAN: Oh, she's lovely. I always wanted curly hair.
TOM: Oh, she's straightened her hair. It's not curly anymore. She doesn't wear glasses now, either.
WOMAN: So now she has straight hair and contact lenses?
TOM Yeah, that's right. And her hair's shorter too. Otherwise, it looks just like her.
WOMAN: Speaking of changes, have you seen Bill lately?
TOM: No, how's he doing?
WOMAN: Really well. I mean, he's lost a lot of weight, you know.
TOM: Oh, that's good. He was putting on weight.
WOMAN: He looks much better. You can especially see it in his face. Much slimmer. Oh, and did you know he shaved off his mustache?
TOM: No! No mustache? I can't imagine Bill without some kind of hair on his face. He had that beard in college and he's had that mustache for, what, ten years?
WOMAN: Yes. I miss it. I hope he grows it back. So tell me some more about your girlfriend. ...

Page 32, Listening Task 2: That's different!

These pictures are not the same. Look at the pictures for 30 seconds. How many differences can you find? Circle them. [*pause*] Now listen. Circle the other differences.

[*Sound of page turning*]
MAN: Look, it's one of those "find the difference" games.
WOMAN: Oh, where the pictures are almost the same?

MAN: Yeah, but there are twenty small differences. Let's try it.
WOMAN: OK. Let's see. Well, the woman's wearing shoes in the top picture.
MAN: Shoes, right. Oh, and glasses. She has glasses in the top picture but not in the bottom one. What else?
WOMAN: Her belt. She's not wearing a belt in the bottom picture. Anything else about her?
MAN: I don't think so. Oh, wait. Look at her hair. It's shorter in the bottom picture.
WOMAN: You're right. She's got shoulder-length hair in the top one. It *is* shorter in the bottom picture.
MAN: I think that's all for her. How about the man?
WOMAN: Well, his shirt is different. He's got a gray shirt on top.
MAN: Yeah, it's white on the bottom.
WOMAN: Oh, and no beard. They shaved off his beard. And his hair is different, isn't it? It's straight in the top picture but curly in the bottom one.
MAN: Right. Oh, and look. He's gotten a bit heavy.
WOMAN: He *is* heavier. Must be those sandwiches.
MAN: Right. Anything else?
WOMAN: Maybe that's all for the man. How about the little girl?
MAN: Well, her hair is darker in the bottom picture. And the shorts. She was wearing jeans before. And …
WOMAN: The glasses are different. She has sunglasses in the first one. Anything else?
MAN: I don't see … wait, there is something. Is she taller in the bottom picture?
WOMAN: Taller? Let me see … yeah, she *is* taller in the bottom picture. Gee, that was hard to notice. You've got good eyes.
MAN: Yeah. Speaking of eyes, look at the little boy. His black eye's moved.
WOMAN: You're right. His left eye is black in the top picture, but it's his right eye in the bottom one.
MAN: What else?
WOMAN: Oh, his shirt is different. He's wearing a long-sleeved shirt in the bottom picture.
MAN: That's right. And look – hair. No, it's his *cap*. He's wearing a cap in the top picture.
WOMAN: Hmm. How about the man who's asleep?
MAN: Gee, he looks the same to me.
WOMAN: Oh, but the jogger. The older man is different. His T-shirt. One says USC and the other is UBC.
MAN: Yeah, the T-shirt. The University of Southern California and the University of British Columbia. That's tricky. Oh, look, his mustache is gone. He doesn't have a mustache in the bottom picture.
WOMAN: You're right. And his nose is bigger.

T14

MAN: Yeah, his nose is bigger. What's different about his hair? It looks ...

WOMAN: Oh, yeah. He has more hair in the top picture. Looks like he's starting to lose his hair in the bottom one.

MAN: Let's see, that's ... 15 ... 16 ... 17 ... 18 ... 19. That's 19. There's one more. I don't ...

WOMAN: Yeah, what's the other change?

MAN: Hmm.

Unit 10 What do you do?

Page 34, Listening Task 1: Who are they talking to?

Listen. Who are these people talking to? Write the occupations on the line. What words helped you know? Write one or two words under each line.

NUMBER 1

MAN: Hi, I'll have the fish ... Ah, that's white fish, right? And, I guess for the vegetable I'd like broccoli. Now, let's see, should I have a potato or rice? I'll have the rice.

NUMBER 2

GIRL: Well, Ms. Wilson, I really did mean to do the homework. I was going to read the chapter and write a report but, uh, well first I lost my book. I couldn't find it all week. Then yesterday someone found it for me. I guess I left it in the cafeteria. I was going to do it last night but when I got home my sister was sick, so I had to take care of her and ...

NUMBER 3

WOMAN: Good morning. These letters need to be typed right away. Oh, and after you type them, make two copies of each. Can you do that before eleven o'clock? I'd like to sign them before my meeting. Also, if you could fax our Manila office and ask when we can expect their report. Also, could you bring the file on the RX accounts? I'd appreciate that file right away. Thanks.

NUMBER 4

MAN: My back really hurts. I thought you should look at it. I was feeling fine till about a week ago. Then I started feeling this pain. It's my lower back. I haven't been doing anything that difficult really, like physical exercise or work or anything. Then the pain started. It doesn't hurt all the time – mostly in the mornings when I get up. I can hardly move.

NUMBER 5

WOMAN: I want to buy some traveler's checks.

Eight hundred dollars' worth. Can I have four hundred in fifty-dollar checks? The rest in twenties? These are American Expense traveler's checks? Good. And I'd like to withdraw the money from my savings account to pay for them.

NUMBER 6

MAN: Eighty! Eighty miles an hour? Come on! I wasn't going eighty. I couldn't have been driving that fast. I must have been driving ... a lot slower than that ... only about sixty miles an hour. Sixty at the most. No. No. Please. Listen, please don't give me a ticket. If I get one more speeding ticket – my license. I'll lose my license. Really, please, I'm really sorry. I really will drive slower. Please?

Page 35, Listening Task 2: I'm going to become a programmer.

Listen. These students are talking about jobs after graduation. What are they going to become? How sure are they? Check "yes," "maybe," or "no" for each profession.

[*Music*]

MARIA: I can't believe this is our last year. College is going by so fast.

KENT: Yeah, we're going to have to face "the real world."

TONY: So, Maria, have you figured out what you're going to do after you graduate? Work with computers?

MARIA: Yeah, I'm going to become a programmer. Dr. Larson, you know, in Computer Science? He thinks I've got a really good chance of getting a job at Apple Computer.

TONY: Wow. The big time.

MARIA: Yeah, but even if I work for a different company, I'll have a good time. I just really enjoy working with computers – seeing how much they can do. How about you, Kent? Are you going to teach art?

KENT: I don't think so. I don't really want to teach. I love art, but teaching is different. I'd like to become an artist. I don't know. It's difficult to find that kind of job.

DIANE: Maybe you could work in advertising.

KENT: Yeah, something like that. But it's almost impossible to get by on your own – you know, just be an independent free-lance artist. But, who knows? Maybe I'll try.

DIANE: Well, I've decided for sure. I'm going to law school. I'm going to be a lawyer.

TONY: You know, Diane, I'm not surprised you want to be a lawyer. But watch, it'll be Diane's first step into politics. Someday, "Ladies and gentlemen, Senator Diane Walker."

DIANE: Politics? Who knows. Maybe, but that won't

be for a few years. First I have to think about law school.

MARIA: So, Tony, are you still planning on going to cooking school?

TONY: Cooking school? It's *culinary* school, Maria. And yes, I'm going to learn to be a chef. I've always liked cooking. I think I've got my plans pretty clear. I'm going to be a chef, work for a few years – you know, learn the restaurant business, then open my own place.

MARIA: You want to be a restaurant owner?

TONY: Oh, I'll own a restaurant, all right. That's the goal.

DIANE: Great, then we'll all meet at your restaurant in ten years.

KENT: For Diane's election party.

Unit 11 What are they talking about?

Page 37, Listening Task 1: I wouldn't ask that.

Listen. What are these people talking about? Circle the topics.

[*Sound of a party, music*]
CARMEN: Lots of people.
PAT: Yeah, there are. Nice party.
CARMEN: Very nice. The food's wonderful.
PAT: Have you tried the shrimp? It's great.
CARMEN: By the way, I'm Carmen. Carmen Lopez
PAT: Nice to meet you, Carmen. I'm Pat Brooks.
CARMEN: What do you do, Pat?
PAT: I work at the university. I'm in the business office. Actually, I'm the office manager. And you?
CARMEN: I work at a bookstore.
[*Music/party sounds*]
ROB: I'm going to get something to drink. Would you like something?
AMY: Ah, yeah. Just a mineral water, I guess.
ROB: OK. Just a minute. [*pause*] Here you are.
AMY: Thanks.
ROB: So Jim said you're new in town.
AMY: Yeah, I just moved here last month. I'm from Toronto originally.
ROB: Toronto? So how do you like it here?
AMY: Oh, I like it a lot.
[*Music/party sounds*]
GREG: Great weather.
MARY: Yeah, it's so warm. I was worried it would rain.
GREG: We were lucky, I guess.
MARY: Um, I don't think we've met. I'm Mary Chang.
GREG: I'm Greg Rogers.
MARY: So, how do you like this music?

GREG: Well, it's OK, I guess. Actually, I wish they'd put on something to dance to.
MARY: That'd be nice.

Look at the topics you circled. Did you check "yes" for these topics in Warming Up? Look at the topics you didn't circle. In English-speaking countries, people don't usually talk about these topics when they first meet.

Page 38, Listening Task 2: A day in the life ...

Listen. Meg and Ted have a lot of different conversations during the day. Who is Meg or Ted talking to? Match each conversation with a picture. Write the number in the box. There is one extra picture. What helped you understand? Write at least one thing for each.

NUMBER 1

MEG: Another cup of coffee? I'd love one, Ted. [*sound of coffee being poured*] Thanks. Oh, you have that meeting with your boss today. Good luck. I hope she likes your proposal. I've got a big day today too. Working on that new contract. Gee, oh, and we have that party tonight. We're supposed to be at the Jeffersons' at seven-thirty. I'll be getting home around six. Should be enough time.

NUMBER 2

TED: Oooh, look who's awake! Hi, sweetheart. You look happy this morning. Let's see, let's get you changed. You want to see Grandma? You like to see Grandma, don't you. Let's go to Grandma's.

NUMBER 3

MEG: Come on, guys, I have to get going. You're going to be late for school and I'm going to be late for work. Let's go. Did you get all your homework done? Don't forget to take your library books either. You help Grandma after school, OK? She needs some help cleaning up the yard.

NUMBER 4

MEG: What are you doing, boy? You want something to eat? Yeah, your bowl's empty. Let's go get some water too. Let's put some water in your bowl. Ah, you're a good boy. Go outside before you eat, OK? [*door opens*] Go on, go outside.

NUMBER 5

TED: Here's the report. I'd like to direct your attention to the last several pages. I've tried to build a case for some quick action about the new system. Now, I'll be meeting the Gold Star people on Wednesday and I hope to get their proposals then ...

NUMBER 6

MEG: Hi, Charles. This is Meg Lowell from the Williams Agency. I'm just fine, thanks. How about you? Great. Listen, the reason I'm calling is that we've got some possibilities on the new contract. They seem good. Perhaps we could arrange a meeting next week. OK. How about Thursday morning, say ten-thirty?

Unit 12 How was your vacation?

Page 40, Listening Task 1: Did you have a good time?

Listen. People are talking about their vacations. Draw lines to the things they did. Did they enjoy themselves? Complete the sentences.

NUMBER 1

LAURA: Hi, Kenji.
KENJI: Laura. Good to see you.
LAURA: Yeah. So how was your vacation?
KENJI: Great. I had a really good time. You knew I went to Vancouver, didn't you?
LAURA: Yeah. How was it? I hear Vancouver's beautiful.
KENJI: Terrific scenery. I went to this fantastic garden.
LAURA: Really? I didn't know you liked gardening.
KENJI: Oh, I don't like gardening. But I love to *look* at gardens. It's a lot less work.
LAURA: That's for sure. So what else did you do?
KENJI: Went to some great restaurants. The seafood there is outstanding.
LAURA: Really?
KENJI: Yeah. Crab, lobster. Great food. Not that expensive, either. It was terrific. So how was your vacation?
LAURA: Well, I didn't go anywhere special. I stayed home.
KENJI: You just relaxed?
LAURA: That's right. I stayed home and did a lot of reading. Read, what, four or five books. I did go to the beach one day and went swimming. But mostly I just took it easy.
KENJI: Oh. Sounds nice.
LAURA: It was nice – very relaxing – but I still wish I had the money to take a trip.

NUMBER 2

DAVE: Did you have a good vacation, Lisa?
LISA: Exciting, really exciting. Diane and I went to Brazil.
DAVE: Wow. Brazil! That does sound exciting. What did you do?
LISA: Well, we flew to Rio and we were really tired, so we spent the first few days on the beach.

DAVE: You flew all that way and just went to the beach?
LISA: Oh, but the beaches there are wonderful. But that wasn't all we did. After that, we flew to the interior of Brazil. It's really beautiful. We visited some old mining areas. We saw some old diamond mines, gold mines …
DAVE: Diamond mines? Did you bring back any souvenirs?
LISA: Sorry, Dave, no gold or diamonds. Then we flew to Brasília, the capital. There are some fantastic buildings there, really modern.
DAVE: Yeah, I've heard about the buildings in Brasília.
LISA: Oh, and the people were so friendly. They were really nice. The food's great too. So, how about you? What did you do on your vacation, Dave?
DAVE: I didn't do much. I just visited relatives.
LISA: How was that?
DAVE: Well, you know. Pretty boring, actually. I like my aunt and uncle, of course. We talked a lot. But after a couple of days there just wasn't much to talk about. So I ended up watching a lot of TV. Yeah, talk and TV. That's about it. Not the most exciting time I've ever had. No, not very exciting at all.
LISA: Oh, that's too bad.

Page 41, Listening Task 2: A weekend to remember (unfortunately)

Listen. Tom went camping last weekend. He didn't have a good time. Put the pictures in order.

FRIEND: Hi, Tom. How was your camping trip last weekend?
TOM: It was a disaster.
FRIEND: A disaster? What was so bad?
TOM: Well, I went camping. But you wouldn't believe the bad luck I had.
FRIEND: Yeah? What happened?
TOM: Well, I went to Pine Hills. I got there Saturday afternoon. And the weather was really nice so I went for a hike.
FRIEND: Yeah?
TOM: You know that big forest there?
FRIEND: Mm-hmm.
TOM: I got lost. I had absolutely no idea where I was.
FRIEND: Lost? That's too bad. So what happened?
TOM: Well, I finally found my way back to the campsite. It was like eight or eight-thirty at night. I was really tired and hungry, so I was going to fix dinner. I'd brought along a nice, juicy steak. I was cooking it over the campfire.
FRIEND: That sounds good.
TOM: Well, yeah, so I cooked it. Well, I tried to

cook it. I really couldn't see much, even with a flashlight. I burned the thing. Burned!

FRIEND: Oh, you burned the steak?

TOM: To a crisp. I could hardly eat it. But anyway, I really didn't mind much because I was so tired I just wanted to get some sleep. So I went to bed early. Then, about eleven o'clock, the people next to me turned on some music and started to have a party. I couldn't get back to sleep.

FRIEND: You must have been angry.

TOM: I was *really* angry! Finally, I went over and asked them to turn down the music. Then about two in the morning it started to rain. I mean it poured.

FRIEND: Oh no!

TOM: Bad enough that there was water in my tent. I had to sleep in the car.

FRIEND: You slept in the car? But you drive that little …

TOM: Yeah, I know.

Not real comfortable. But that's not all. I got up in the morning and I found my food was gone.

FRIEND: What happened to it?

TOM: Animals, I guess. Foxes or raccoons, probably. I had put the food in the tent, but they got it. So I had no breakfast. By that time I figured the weekend was ruined anyway, so I decided to leave.

FRIEND: Yeah.

TOM: But my car was stuck. There was so much rain that I was stuck in the mud. I finally found a ranger to help push me out.

FRIEND: This doesn't sound like a camping trip to be repeated.

TOM: That's for sure. Oh, and to finish it off, I had a flat tire on the way home.

FRIEND: A flat tire? Gee, I don't imagine you're going camping again for a while.

TOM: Oh, I don't know. I might go again next weekend.

FRIEND: What?

TOM: Hey, nobody could have that kind of bad luck two weeks in a row.

Unit 13 Around the house

Page 43, Listening Task 1: I hate doing that!

Listen. People are talking about jobs around the house and other chores. Do they like them or dislike them? Draw lines to show how strongly they feel.

NUMBER 1: Cooking

[*Sound of supermarket; carts*]

BOB: Oh, Jim. Hi. You shop here too?

JIM: Usually.

BOB: Hey, I picked up some steaks. You free Saturday night?

JIM: Saturday? Yeah.

BOB: Why don't you come over? We can barbecue.

JIM: That sounds good. Thanks. Gee, I didn't know you liked cooking.

BOB: Well, I'm not really a fan of cooking. It's just something you do. We've all got to eat.

JIM: True. So what time?

BOB: Oh, about seven-thirty.

JIM: Can I bring anything? Chips …

NUMBER 2: Washing floors

WIFE: These floors are really dirty. Maybe we should wash them this weekend.

HUSBAND: I really hate washing floors.

WIFE: Well, they're not going to get clean by themselves.

HUSBAND: OK, OK. Look – I have an idea. If you wash the floors, I'll do the dishes, uh, every night next week. All week.

WIFE: Hmm. Dishes all week. And what else?

NUMBER 3: Giving the baby a bath

[*Phone rings; pick up*]

CHUCK: Hello.

DAVE: Hi, Chuck. This is Dave. Listen. I'm calling about the car pool.

CHUCK: Oh, yeah. Listen, Dave, I was just about to give the baby a bath. Can I call you back in about a half an hour?

DAVE: Oh, sure. You've got to bathe the baby. Sounds like work.

CHUCK: No, it's great. Kent loves the water. Bath time is usually loads of fun. We really enjoy it. Anyway, I'll call you back in a little while.

DAVE: OK. I'll talk to you in a bit. Bye.

CHUCK: Bye. [*hangs up*]

NUMBER 4: Doing laundry

CARRIE: Jan, I'm doing the laundry. Do you have anything you need washed?

JAN: Uh, yeah. Just a couple of shirts. You really don't mind washing clothes, do you?

CARRIE: Naw, its OK. Now that we have a washing machine, it's no problem at all.

JAN: You sound like a television commercial.

CARRIE: No, it's not that I *love* doing laundry. But with our washer I don't have to waste time sitting in a Laundromat. So, I don't know, it's no problem. I don't mind it at all.

JAN: Yeah, I can see that. Anyway, thanks.

NUMBER 5: Washing dishes

[*Dishes clanging*]

SUE: So, let's see. It's your turn to wash dishes, right?

JILL: Wait, is it? But I made dinner.
SUE: Come on. We decided to switch every other day.
JILL: Yeah, but ...
SUE: Jill!
JILL: Yeah, OK.

NUMBER 6: Cleaning the office
[*Sound of papers being shuffled*]
FRIEND: You know, Marc, this office is really a mess.
MARC: Yeah, well, I've been very busy.
FRIEND: Yeah, but still. How can you find things?
MARC: I know where things are. Cleaning is such a pain. I mean, I do clean sometimes. But, you know, like, you take a day to really clean – you know, put everything away and clean the desk and straighten the files and really clean. And then, what, six months later, you've got to do the whole thing again.
FRIEND: You're hopeless.

Page 44, Listening Task 2: I agree!
Listen. Does the man like these things? Check "likes" or "dislikes." Why? Write his reasons.

NUMBER 1: Working at home
[*Doorbell rings; door opens*]
AL: Sue! Come on in.
SUE: Hi Al. I brought a little something for your new house.
AL: A plant. Gee, thanks.
SUE: Nice house. It's so big.
AL: Yeah, we're very happy here. My wife and I are both going to work at home, you know. Work on the computer, fax things in ...
SUE: Work at home! I'd love to do that. No more driving to work; no traffic. And the office is always so noisy. I can't seem to work well there.
AL: Well, my office wasn't that noisy, but it'll be even quieter here. I can think about what I'm doing. And not driving during rush hour – that's a plus. Anyway, let me show you the house. Here's the kitchen. This is what really excites me about the house. It's my favorite room ...

NUMBER 2: Cooking
SUE: You're such a good cook.
AL: Well, I *do* like cooking. It's really relaxing after work.
SUE: I guess it can be relaxing if you're good at it. Anyway, I hope you'll have a lot of dinner parties.
AL: Oh, we will.

NUMBER 3: Reading nonfiction
SUE: Look at all these boxes! It looks like you still have some unpacking to do.
AL: Oh, those. Those are my books. I'm going to

build some bookshelves in here, so I haven't unpacked them yet.
SUE: All these are books? Wow! You must love to read.
AL: Yeah, I do. Nonfiction mostly – biographies, history, current events, that kind of thing. I feel like I really learn a lot that way. I'm not crazy about fiction. I don't know – it usually bores me. But nonfiction I like. I learn a lot.
SUE: Yeah, I can see that.

NUMBER 4: Growing flowers
AL: Outside there's enough room for a garden.
SUE: Are you going to grow flowers?
AL: No, I don't like growing flowers. It's not worth the work. I think I want to grow vegetables – tomatoes, corn, beans, green peppers, everything. If you grow them yourself, they taste much better than they do when you buy them in a store.
SUE: Yeah, vegetables from the supermarket have no taste. Homegrown ones are better.

NUMBER 5: Driving
AL: I haven't figured out what to do with the garage. Did I tell you we sold our car?
SUE: You sold your car? You don't need one?
AL: Not really. I've never liked driving, anyway. I hate traffic. And now we live close to all the stores. Most of our friends live close by too. And it's only a ten-minute walk to the train station. We just don't need a car.
SUE: Ten minutes to the station? That's not bad.
AL: Yeah, well ... So let's go back inside.

Do you agree with Al's opinions? Circle "I agree" or "I don't agree."

Unit 14 Shopping

Page 46, Listening Task 1: It's perfect!
Listen. Some people are shopping. What are they buying? Match each conversation with a picture. Write the number in the box. There are three extra pictures.

NUMBER 1
[*Sound of a department store*]
SHOPPER: Do you have any of the smaller ones on sale?
CLERK: I'm afraid only the twenty-seven-inch model is on sale, sir.
SHOPPER: It's really a little bigger than I wanted. You see, I don't really watch it much, but you know, sometimes for the news and all.
CLERK: Right.
SHOPPER: How about this one? The portable one.

CLERK: Well, that one's twenty dollars more.
SHOPPER: That's OK. I want something small. I
just watch the news. And football sometimes.
CLERK: OK, then, the portable one.

NUMBER 2
FIRST SHOPPER: What do you think? Big enough?
SECOND SHOPPER: Oh, it's plenty big. Your
apartment's not that big, anyway.
FIRST SHOPPER: That's something to think about.
Too big?
SECOND SHOPPER: Well, it would seat four
people with no problem.
FIRST SHOPPER: Well, that's a nice size for a party.
SECOND SHOPPER: True. Do you ever invite more
people over for dinner?
FIRST SHOPPER: Sometimes, but not very often.
SECOND SHOPPER: Well then, this is big enough.
This and four chairs? Look at …

NUMBER 3
SHOPPER: How old is this one?
SALESMAN: That one is only three years old. It's in
great condition.
SHOPPER: I really don't like the color.
SALESMAN: Really? You don't like yellow-green?
SHOPPER: No, I really don't. Besides, I drive to
work with three other people. Maybe I need
something a little bigger.
SALESMAN: How about this blue one? It's a nice
bright color, and it has a big back seat. It was
owned by an older gentleman who …

NUMBER 4
FIRST SHOPPER: Look at these. What an ugly
color. They're terrible! What were the designers
thinking about?
SECOND SHOPPER : I don't know – I kind of like
the color.
FIRST SHOPPER: Really? With those bright blue
laces?
SECOND SHOPPER: Yeah, in fact, I'm going to try
them on.
FIRST SHOPPER: Go ahead. Maybe they'll look
good on you.
SECOND SHOPPER: There – I've got them on. Not
bad.
FIRST SHOPPER: They make your feet look a little
big.
SECOND SHOPPER: You're right. My feet are big
enough already. Well, how about these gray ones
with the low heel?
FIRST SHOPPER: Hmm, the gray ones. Now *they're*
nice.

NUMBER 5
CLERK: May I help you?
SHOPPER: Yes, do you have these in a smaller size?

CLERK: I'm sorry. That's the only size in blue. We
have some brown ones.
SHOPPER: I have a blue jacket I want to wear them
with. These would really go with the jacket.
CLERK: I'm sorry, sir. Could I show you some
others?
SHOPPER: How about some jeans, instead?

Page 47, Listening Task 2: I'll take it.
Listen. People are shopping. Do you think they will
buy these things? Circle "yes" or "no." When the
answer is "no," write the reason.

NUMBER 1: The jacket
SHOPPER: Excuse me. I like this jacket, but … um,
do you have any different designs?
CLERK: No, sir, actually, striped is the only style we
have.
SHOPPER: Really?
CLERK: Yes, stripes are very popular this year.
SHOPPER: Oh. Well, thank you. Maybe I'll look
around a bit more.
CLERK: That's fine, sir.

NUMBER 2: The CD player
CLERK: May I help you?
SHOPPER: Yeah, how much is the CD player?
CLERK: Let's see … Oh, it's on sale right now. It's
only eighty-five ninety-nine.
SHOPPER: Wow, that's cheap.
CLERK: Yes, it's a very good buy.
SHOPPER: Hmm.

NUMBER 3: The cordless phone
FIRST SHOPPER: Gee, look at this. A cordless
phone for less than fifty dollars.
SECOND SHOPPER: That's really cheap. We've
talked about getting a cordless phone. It sure
would be convenient. What brand is it?
FIRST SHOPPER: Brand? Uh, let's see. It's Electo.
SECOND SHOPPER: Electo? Have you ever heard
of it?
FIRST SHOPPER: Hmm. No, I haven't.
SECOND SHOPPER: I don't know. With electronic
stuff, if you don't know the company that made
it …
FIRST SHOPPER: Yeah, I know what you mean.

NUMBER 4: The jeans
FIRST SHOPPER: [*footsteps*] So, what do you think?
SECOND SHOPPER: They look great on you, Sue.
FIRST SHOPPER: Yeah, the fit's good. But I always
worry with jeans. The cotton might shrink.
SECOND SHOPPER: Hmm, yeah, wash them a few
times and they might be too small.
FIRST SHOPPER: Maybe they have a bigger size.
[*speaking to Clerk*] Excuse me.

CLERK: Yes?

FIRST SHOPPER: Do you have these in the next larger size?

CLERK: Let me check, ma'am. Ah, I'm sorry. We don't seem to have that size at the moment.

NUMBER 5: The computer

FIRST SHOPPER: There are so many different kinds of computers – I don't know which to buy.

SECOND SHOPPER: Well, what are you going to use it for?

FIRST SHOPPER: Well, just my own writing mainly. You know, I'm working on a novel.

SECOND SHOPPER: How's it going?

FIRST SHOPPER: Pretty good, actually.

SECOND SHOPPER: Well, are you going to write at home, or when you travel, or … when?

FIRST SHOPPER: Well, I do travel a lot. Maybe I'll think about a laptop.

SECOND SHOPPER: I'm really happy with mine. It's wonderful.

FIRST SHOPPER: Yeah? Really convenient?

SECOND SHOPPER: It's easy to use. And so lightweight. I love mine.

FIRST SHOPPER: Hmm. [*sound of someone keyboarding*] This laptop is certainly easy to use. Maybe I'll …

NUMBER 6: The notebook

SHOPPER: Excuse me.

CLERK: Yes?

SHOPPER: Are these all the notebooks you have?

CLERK: Yes. Is there something special you're looking for?

SHOPPER: These all seem to have fifty pages. Uh, do you have any with more pages? Like a hundred or maybe a hundred and fifty?

CLERK: I'm sorry. All the notebooks we have are right there.

SHOPPER: Oh, I see. I'll guess I'll keep looking. Thanks.

Unit 15 Going places

Page 49, Listening Task 1: How much do you know?

Listen. You are going to take a "quiz" on countries. Look at the map. Which countries is the speaker talking about? Write the numbers in the boxes. What information helped you guess each country? Write your answers.

NUMBER 1

QUIZ READER: This country is just north of the equator. It produces oil. It is in South America. The people of this country speak Spanish. [pause]

What's number one? It's a South American country just north of the equator. It produces a lot of oil. The people speak Spanish.

NUMBER 2

QUIZ READER: This country is in the Northern Hemisphere. Its culture is very old. This country is in Asia, southwest of China. The people there speak many languages, including English, Hindi, and Bengali. [*pause*] What's number two? It's in the Northern Hemisphere, southwest of China. The culture is very old. More than eight hundred languages are spoken there.

NUMBER 3

QUIZ READER: This country is also in Asia. It is a country of many islands. Most of the country is below the equator. It is north of Australia. The capital city is Jakarta. [*pause*] Do you know number three? This Asian country is made up of over thirteen thousand islands. Most of it is below the equator. It's located just north of Australia. The capital is Jakarta.

NUMBER 4

QUIZ READER: This country has a very long history. The country is on the Mediterranean Sea. The country is in southern Europe. It is shaped like a boot. [*pause*] What is number four? It's located in southern Europe, on the Mediterranean Sea, and looks like a boot.

NUMBER 5

QUIZ READER: This country is in Africa. It is above the equator. It is not in western Africa. The Nile River is in this country. [*pause*] Which country is number five? It's in northeastern Africa, above the equator. The Nile River runs through it.

NUMBER 6

QUIZ READER: This country is in Asia, in the Northern Hemisphere. It's an island country. Many languages, including Tagalog, English, and Spanish are spoken in this country. Its capital is Manila. [*pause*] Many languages are spoken in country number six. It's an island country in the Northern Hemisphere. Its capital is Manila.

NUMBER 7

QUIZ READER: This country is on the equator. Most of the country is south of the equator. This country has beaches on the Atlantic Ocean. It has the largest population in South America. The biggest cities are São Paulo and Rio de Janeiro. [*pause*] What is number seven? São Paulo and Rio de Janeiro are the largest cities. The country, known for its beautiful beaches, has the largest population in South America.

QUIZ READER: Number eight is in the Northern Hemisphere. This country produces oil, machines, and food. Its capital is the largest city in North America. The main language is Spanish. [*pause*] Can you guess number eight? Located in North America, this Spanish-speaking country is known for its oil, machinery, and food products. The capital is one of the largest cities in the world.

Page 50, Listening Task 2: Game show

Listen. Two people are playing a TV game show. What are the correct answers? Write each country or place. Who gets the points? Check "X" for the woman's points. Check "O" for the man's points.

[*Music followed by applause*]

VANCE: Good evening, everyone, and welcome to Travel Trivia, the show that shows who knows what about the world. I'm your host Vance Wilson and tonight our contestants are Jane Thomas and Mike Rogers. Welcome, Jane and Mike.

JANE: Hi, Vance.

MIKE: Hello, Vance.

VANCE: Now, to win the game you must get three squares in a row – up, down, or across. Jane, you're first. Which question do you want?

JANE: I'll take the middle, question number five.

VANCE: OK, question five: Which has more people, Taiwan or Thailand?

JANE: Hmm ... Thailand?

VANCE: Thailand is correct! Let's put an "X" there. [*ding*] Mike, it's your turn.

MIKE: How about number one, Vance?

VANCE: Number one it is. OK, Mike, which has more people, Latin America or Europe?

MIKE: Latin America has more. [*buzzer*]

VANCE: Sorry, Mike, it's not Latin America. Europe has more people. So, let's put an "X" there. [*ding*] Jane, it's your turn.

JANE: I'll take number nine, Vance.

VANCE: Number nine to win. Now, Jane, for the game, which Latin American country produces the most cars? Is it Brazil, Mexico, or Argentina?

JANE: Mexico makes a lot of cars.

VANCE: [*buzzer*] Yes, Mexico makes a lot but Brazil makes the most cars. Brazil. Mike's point. Put an "O" in that square. [*ding*] Mike, which question?

MIKE: How about three.

VANCE: And number three it is. Mike, which is bigger, France or Spain?

MIKE: France.

VANCE: Right you are. France is bigger than Spain. That's an "O." [*ding*] Jane?

JANE: Number six to block.

VANCE: And question six is: Which is farther south, Tokyo or Madrid?

JANE: Oh, I know this one. Tokyo. Tokyo is farther south.

VANCE: That's right. And an "X" marks the spot. [*ding*] Mike?

MIKE: Uh, number four?

VANCE: Question four. OK, Mike, which country – the United States, Sweden, or Taiwan – has the highest percentage of working women?

MIKE: Working women? Um, I'll guess ... Sweden?

VANCE: And Sweden it is! Let's put a circle in square four. [*ding*] Jane, it's your turn.

JANE: Number two, please.

VANCE: OK, Jane. Question two is about cities in the Arab world. Which Arab city has the largest population?

JANE: Um. Cairo, I think.

VANCE: Well, you think right. Cairo is the largest Arab city. Put an "X" there. [*ding*] Mike, you'd better block.

MIKE: I'll take number eight to block.

VANCE: Question number eight is: Which U.S. state is the farthest south? Is it Texas, Florida, or Hawaii?

MIKE: Farthest south? Let's see. Miami is ... or is it ... ? I'll say ... Florida! [*buzzer*]

VANCE: Well, you should have said Hawaii. Because Hawaii is the farthest south! [*ding*] And that makes Jane our champion, and the winner of a trip to the Aloha state. Congratulations, Jane! [*applause, music*]

Unit 16 Making plans

[*Phone rings; pickup*]

KAREN: Hello.

TONY: Hi, Karen. This is Tony.

KAREN: Oh, hi. I'm looking forward to lunch tomorrow.

TONY: Uh, that's what I'm calling about. We were supposed to meet at noon, right?

KAREN: Yeah. Um, at the Bangkok Cafe.

TONY: Look, we're kind of busy here at work. Can we have lunch a little closer to my office? I have to get right back to my desk.

KAREN: Yeah, OK. How about the Plaza?

TONY: The Plaza? Great! I love their salad bar.

KAREN: OK. I'll see you at the Plaza at noon then.

TONY: OK. Sorry about the change, Karen.

KAREN: Oh, no problem.

TONY: Bye.

KAREN: Bye. [*hangs up*]

FIRST WOMAN: So we're meeting at seven-thirty in front of Hayes Hall, right?

SECOND WOMAN: Well, how about earlier? Would you like to get something to eat before the concert?

FIRST WOMAN: That'd be nice. Let's go to the Museum Cafe.

SECOND WOMAN: OK. About six-thirty?

FIRST WOMAN: Ah, well. Let's meet at six. Give ourselves a little more time. We don't want to be late for the concert.

SECOND WOMAN: Six, at the Museum Cafe. Got it. No problem.

NUMBER 3

ANNOUNCER: Attention passengers on Northern Airways flight 475 to Seattle. There has been a delay. The flight will now depart at six o'clock. Flight 475 to Seattle will leave at six o'clock from gate twelve.

PASSENGER: Six o'clock! Great. We've got some time. Let's get something to eat.

NUMBER 4

[*Phone rings; pickup*]

PATIENT: Hello.

SECRETARY: Hello. Ms. Clark?

PATIENT: Yes.

SECRETARY: This is Dr. Lee's office. You have an appointment today at two-thirty.

PATIENT: Yes, that's right.

SECRETARY: We're very sorry, but Dr. Lee was called to the hospital today. We'd like to reschedule your appointment to tomorrow at the same time.

PATIENT: Tomorrow at two-thirty? That's the twenty-first?

SECRETARY: That's right. Tomorrow at two-thirty.

PATIENT: That's OK.

SECRETARY: We're sorry for the inconvenience.

PATIENT: That's all right. Goodbye.

SECRETARY: Bye.

Page 53, Listening Task 2: Monday morning!

Listen. A secretary is taking telephone messages. Write the changes on the schedule.

[*Phone rings; pickup*]

SECRETARY: Good morning, Dr. Porter's office.

MR. LONG: Good morning. I have an appointment with Dr. Porter at ten-thirty. I'm running a little late. Could I reschedule for eleven-thirty?

SECRETARY: That's Mr. Long?

MR. LONG: That's right.

SECRETARY: OK, let me move you to eleven-thirty, Mr. Long. [*sound of writing*] Eleven-thirty. Mr. Long.

MR. LONG: Thank you very much.

SECRETARY: You're welcome. [*phone rings; answers*] Dr. Porter's office.

MS. WELLS: This is Virginia Wells. I'm feeling awful. Could I see Dr. Porter today?

SECRETARY: Let's see … would you like a morning or afternoon appointment?

MS. WELLS: I'd like to get in as soon as possible. Any time after ten o'clock.

SECRETARY: We've just had a cancellation for 10:30. [*phone rings*] Could you hold on, Ms. Wells? [*answers phone*] Dr. Porter's office, good morning.

MS. PARK: This is S. H. Park. Dr. Porter told me to call about my test results.

SECRETARY: Could you hold, Ms. Park?

MS. PARK: Yes.

SECRETARY: Thank you. [*switches lines*] Hello? Ms. Wells? Sorry to keep you waiting. Would you like the ten-thirty appointment?

MS. WELLS: Yes, please.

SECRETARY: That's fine. [*sound of writing*] Ten-thirty, Ms. Wells. We'll see you then. [*switches lines*] Thank you for waiting, Ms. Park. The doctor will be in at about nine-thirty. Can I have her call you then?

MS. PARK: She'll call at about nine-thirty? That's fine.

SECRETARY: OK. Let me make a note of that. [*sound of writing*] Call Ms. Park at nine-thirty. OK, Ms. Park. She'll call at nine-thirty. I'll let her know as soon as she gets here. Goodbye. [*phone rings; answers*] Good morning, Dr. Porter's office.

MS. GREEN: This is Ellen Green. I'd like an appointment today.

SECRETARY: We have an opening at three-thirty, Ms. Green. How's that?

MS. GREEN: Three-thirty? I'll be there. I feel awful.

SECRETARY: That's Ms. Green at three-thirty.

MS. GREEN: Thanks a lot.

SECRETARY: You're welcome. Goodbye. [*hangs up*] I'm beginning to feel pretty sick myself. [*phone rings*] Dr. Porter's office.

MR. FRANKS: This is Tom Franks. I have an appointment at twelve-thirty today. I'd like to cancel it.

SECRETARY: Twelve-thirty. Cancel Mr. Franks. OK. Would you like to reschedule, Mr. Franks?

MR. FRANKS: No, not right now. I'll make another appointment later. [*phone rings*]

SECRETARY: Fine, thanks for calling. [*switches lines*] Good morning, Dr. Porter's office.

DR. PORTER: Morning, Stella.

SECRETARY: Oh, Dr. Porter.

DR. PORTER: Yes. I've been trying to call you but the lines have been very busy. Anyway, I'm feeling very sick this morning. I really can't come in. Could you call today's patients and let them know?

SECRETARY: Cancel all patients? Sure, Doctor. Take care of yourself.

DR. PORTER: Thanks, Stella.
SECRETARY: I hope you feel better. Goodbye.
DR. PORTER: Bye.

Unit 17 Youth culture

Page 55, Listening Task 1: Jeans

Read this story. Now listen. There are ten mistakes.
The tape is correct. Find the mistakes. Write the
correct information.

READER: Jeans: The "Uniform" of Youth
     Jeans are very popular with young people all over
the world. Some people say that jeans are almost the
"uniform" of youth. But they haven't always been
popular.
     The story of jeans started almost two hundred
years ago. People in Genoa, Italy, made pants. The
cloth made in Genoa was called "jeanos." The pants
were called "jeans." In 1850, a salesman in California
began selling pants made of canvas. His name was
Levi Strauss. Because they were so strong, "Levi's
pants" became popular with gold miners, farmers,
and cowboys. Six years later, Levi began making his
pants with a blue cotton cloth called denim. Soon
after, factory workers in the United States and
Europe began wearing jeans. Young people usually
didn't wear them.
     In the 1950s, two people helped make jeans
popular with teenagers: Elvis Presley, the king of
rock and roll, and James Dean, a famous movie star.
Elvis wore tight jeans. Most parents didn't like Elvis
or his music. But teenagers loved him and started to
dress like him. In *Rebel Without a Cause*, James Dean
wore jeans. He was a hero to many young people.
     During the 1960s, rock and roll became even
more popular. Young people had more freedom.
Their clothes showed their independence. Some
people decorated their jeans with colorful patches
and flowers.
     In the seventies and eighties, jeans became very
expensive. In addition to the regular brands like
Levi's and Lee, famous designers like Calvin Klein
and Pierre Cardin began making "designer jeans."
They were very stylish and very expensive.
     Jeans are so popular that Levi's has sold over
twenty billion pairs. Almost anywhere in the world
you know what young people want to wear: jeans!

Page 56, Listening Task 2: Rock and roll!

Look at the covers of the CDs. Do you know
anything about these types of popular music? Listen.
A music expert is talking about the history of
popular music. When did each type of music

become popular? Write the dates on the lines. Write
one or more facts about each type.

[*Music*]
HOST: Good evening and welcome to *Book Talk*.
     Tonight's guest is rock journalist Bruce Stone.
     Bruce has written the best-selling book, *Our Lives,
     Our Music*. It's a history of popular music. Tell us,
     Bruce, when did rock and roll get its start?
BRUCE: Well, you can't put an exact date on it
     because rock grew out of several other types of
     music: especially rhythm and blues, gospel, as well
     as country. But by the mid-1950s we had a distinct
     type of music called rock and roll.
HOST: Where did the name "rock and roll" come
     from? I seem to remember something about a disc
     jockey.
BRUCE: You're probably thinking about Alan
     Freed. He didn't actually invent the name "rock
     and roll." It had been used on rhythm and blues
     radio stations for a number of years. But he did
     make the term popular.
HOST: So in the middle of the 1950s, rock and roll
     was getting popular. Radio was important in
     promoting it, wasn't it?
BRUCE: Absolutely. Radio was extremely important
     in letting millions of young people hear Elvis
     Presley, Chuck Berry, and all the other stars.
HOST: I know there were lots of other early
     rockers, but this is a short show, so let's get to the
     sixties.
BRUCE: Well, one of the most important styles in
     the early sixties was Motown. Motown was very
     popular. The music came from black performers
     based in Detroit. Before the early sixties, many
     radio stations didn't play music by black musicians.
     Once the Motown sound hit, the music was
     everywhere.
HOST: Hmm. And it was just after that that the
     British groups became important, right?
BRUCE: Popular music really changed in the mid-
     1960s. We had the rise of all those British groups.
     By about 1964 or '65, these groups were huge.
HOST: Like the Beatles, the Rolling Stones …
BRUCE: Yeah. Of course, the Beatles and the
     Rolling Stones were the most important, but there
     were a lot of other British groups. London was the
     center for fashion and youth culture in general.
     British music was popular all over the world. Even
     though there were many important American
     bands, they were all influenced by the British.
HOST: What do you see as the next important
     movement?
BRUCE: I'd have to say disco. By the mid-1970s,
     disco was the sound. And, while most young
     people were dancing and romancing to the disco

beat, a lot of hard rock fans hated disco. There was even a rally in Chicago where they destroyed disco albums.

HOST: How about the end of the seventies?

BRUCE: That was the beginning of punk. By the late seventies the music scene had changed a lot. Punk was getting really big, you know. It started in London. New York was a big center for punk too. Some people say that heavy metal music is a continuation of punk, but I don't really think so. Maybe it's because I don't like heavy metal.

HOST: I remember punk well – being in New York in the late seventies, all the clubs. The strange way of dressing …

BRUCE: Yeah, it was weird. Then, by the early 1980s, it was heavy metal. The groups were famous for their leather clothes and their wild performances. A lot of people, well, especially parents, hated heavy metal.

HOST: And then, in the mid-eighties, we started hearing rap.

BRUCE: That's right. Rap music has been really important since the middle of the eighties. Lots of people, not just rappers, use rap in their music. Rap is popular all over the world. That's a little surprising since the words are so hard to understand.

HOST: That's true. There is a lot of slang in rap music.

BRUCE: Heavy metal and rap probably sold the most records during the early nineties, but my favorite music during the early nineties was worldbeat.

HOST: Worldbeat? I don't know much about that.

BRUCE: Well, it's a silly name, really. It just means that people started listening to the music – the beat – from all over the world: from Africa, from Brazil … music in different languages. Even if they didn't understand the words, they loved the music.

HOST: Worldbeat … world music. That is interesting. Hmm. Well, it looks like we're out of time. Thanks for coming to the show.

BRUCE: My pleasure.

HOST: We've been talking to music journalist Bruce Stone, author of *Our Lives, Our Music.* That's it for *Book Talk* this week. [*music*]

Unit 18 Making a difference

Page 58, Listening Task 1: Little things help.

Look at the pictures. What could you do with these things to help the earth? [*pause*] Now listen. People are talking about improving the environment. What do they do with these things? Fill in the blanks.

NUMBER 1: Newspapers

[*Sound of newspapers being stacked for recycling*]

MAN: If you're done reading the newspaper, I'll throw it out.

WOMAN: No, wait. I want to recycle it.

MAN: Recycle the newspaper? That's a good idea.

WOMAN: Yeah, um, just put it in the closet. When we get a big pile, we'll take it to the recycling center.

MAN: OK.

NUMBER 2: Cups

FIRST MAN: Hi, Bob. Do you want a cup of coffee?

SECOND MAN: Yeah, just a minute. My cup's on my desk.

FIRST MAN: That's OK. We've got Styrofoam cups.

SECOND MAN: No, let me get my cup. I don't use Styrofoam cups anymore.

FIRST MAN: Really? Why not?

SECOND MAN: Well, I was reading … Did you know that foam cups *never* break down? They never break down at all. They aren't biodegradable. If I used a Styrofoam cup today, it would still be around in five hundred years. So I use my own cup.

FIRST MAN: Wow! I didn't know that.

NUMBER 3: Bags

[*Sound of cash register totaling a bill*]

CLERK: OK. With tax, that comes to twenty-eight nineteen.

CUSTOMER: Twenty-eight nineteen. OK, here's thirty.

CLERK: And your change. Would you like paper bags or plastic bags?

CUSTOMER: Neither. I brought my own bags.

CLERK: Your own bags?

CUSTOMER: Yes, I've got these cloth bags. I always bring my own shopping bags. Saves trees, you know.

CLERK: Yeah, I suppose it does.

NUMBER 4: Plastic bottles

[*Sound of a plastic bottle being thrown into the garbage*]

WOMAN: Uh, don't throw away that plastic bottle. You can reuse it.

MAN: An old plastic bottle? What for?

WOMAN: To save water. You put some rocks in the bottle and fill it with water. The rocks and water make the bottle heavy. You put the bottle in the bathroom … ah, in the toilet tank.

MAN: You put it in the toilet tank?

WOMAN: Yeah, it saves water. Every time you flush the tank you save fifteen to twenty percent of the water.

MAN: It saves that much water? Wow!

NUMBER 5: An air pressure gauge

FIRST MAN: What's this thing?

SECOND MAN: That? That's an air pressure gauge. You use it to see if there's enough air in your tires.

FIRST MAN: Oh, I've never seen one like this before.

SECOND MAN: Yeah. I've started checking the air pressure in my tires every couple of weeks. Did you know that if your tires are low, your car uses a lot more gasoline?

FIRST MAN: Hmm. I never thought about that.

SECOND MAN: Yeah. So with a two-dollar air gauge, I use less gas and save money.

Page 59, Listening Task 2: Recycling

Listen to this radio announcement. How much of these materials do people in the United States use? Fill in the blanks.

ANNOUNCER: Recycling saves. It saves money, energy, and natural resources. Consider the facts: Aluminum cans are very easy to recycle. But, every three months, we throw away enough aluminum to rebuild all of the commercial airplanes in the country. Yes, every three months, we could take all the aluminum cans we throw away and rebuild all the airplanes for all of the airlines in the country. Please think of that the next time you throw away a soda can.

And we throw away enough iron and steel to supply all of our car makers. If we recycled more metal, our automobile makers would never need any new iron and steel.

Every week, more than five hundred thousand trees are used to make newspapers. Imagine five hundred thousand trees. And two-thirds of those newspapers are thrown away.

This year, we'll throw away enough office and writing paper to build a wall twelve feet high – that's three and a half meters. And that wall would be so long it would go from Los Angeles to New York. Imagine these papers, one on top of another, stacked twelve feet – three and a half meters – in a wall running all the way across the United States.

Every year, we throw away twenty-four million tons of leaves and grass clippings. Twenty-four million tons. Those leaves and grass take up space. They could be composted, allowed to rot or decay so that they could become fertilizer for soil. Compost helps farmers make soil better and richer.

We throw away enough glass bottles to fill the two tallest buildings in New York City every two weeks. Think of it, New York's tallest buildings, filled up like trash cans, full of glass bottles – every two weeks. Those bottles could be recycled.

We throw away two and a half million plastic bottles every hour. Very few plastic bottles are ever recycled. Two and a half million bottles every hour – wasted!

This message is from the Environmental Concern Fund, which reminds you …

If you're not recycling [*clank of glass being thrown into the garbage*], you're throwing it all away.

Unit 19 It's in the news.

Page 61, Listening Task 1: What are they talking about?

Listen. People are talking about newspaper articles. What is the order of the stories? Number the pictures. Write extra facts about each story. There are two extra pictures.

NUMBER 1

[*Sound of newspaper page turning*]

MAN: He's got to be joking.

WOMAN: What's that?

MAN: You know Jerry Ward, the rock musician?

WOMAN: Yeah, the one with the pink hair?

MAN: That's the guy. Remember the strike last year? He had that rally with the doctors and nurses.

WOMAN: Oh, yeah, the rally during the hospital strike. So what about Jerry Ward?

MAN: He's running for mayor. He wants to run the city.

WOMAN: Jerry Ward? You're kidding.

MAN: Look at the paper: "Rock Star Runs for Mayor."

WOMAN: Oh, that's great! Run the city? Just what we need, a pink-haired mayor. I can't believe it.

NUMBER 2

WOMAN: Well they're at it again.

MAN: What do you mean?

WOMAN: Oh, there's that trade meeting in Paris. The industrialized countries are still arguing over trade. This time it's farm products. It's here in the paper.

MAN: Let's see: "Countries Argue Over Farm Product Imports." Arguing over farm imports? It seems like this disagreement has been going on for years.

WOMAN: Yeah, really. Farm products this time. I wonder why they go on with these meetings. They never seem to agree on anything.

NUMBER 3

WOMAN: All right! Did you see the sports page?

MAN: You don't have to tell me. I heard it on the radio.

WOMAN: Come on. Just look at the paper. The game in Vancouver? The Vancouver Bulldogs won! *"The Vancouver Bulldogs Beat the Wildcats."* Those Bulldogs are one great baseball team.

MAN: Yeah, yeah, I heard it.

WOMAN: One great ball club. They haven't lost any games yet. They're undefeated!

MAN: Undefeated. Right.

WOMAN: Think of it. Every other team has lost at least one game. But the Bulldogs haven't.

MAN: No losses. Yeah. I'm going to get another cup of coffee. You want one?

WOMAN: Don't change the subject. *"Bulldogs Down Wildcats!"* I'm so excited!

MAN: I know.

NUMBER 4

WOMAN: What's so funny?

MAN: Did you see this story? The one called "Airline Pilot Locked Out"?

WOMAN: No. What happened?

MAN: Listen to this: "Passengers on a Transglobal Airlines flight, while waiting for take-off at the airport, were surprised by a loud banging on the plane's door."

WOMAN: A banging on the door?

MAN: "When the crew checked, they found the plane's captain, who had been locked out."

WOMAN: The pilot was locked out? That's a good one. What happened then?

MAN: Not much. It just says the plane took off ten minutes late.

WOMAN: Only ten minutes late? Pilot locked out. Sounds like the kind of airline I wouldn't go near. Maybe my fear of flying isn't so crazy.

MAN: Yeah.

Page 62, Listening Task 2: The six o'clock news

Read these newspaper stories. Then listen to the news on the radio. Write the missing information. The type of information you need is in blue.

[*Music*]

ANCHOR: Good evening, and welcome to the six o'clock news. Today's top story is the meeting of the G7 in Paris. The Group of Seven, leaders of the largest industrialized nations, are meeting this week to discuss trade issues. The major issue is farm policy. Our correspondent Sarah Flint is in Paris.

SARAH: The big topic in Paris this week is trade. The leaders of the seven major industrialized nations met today to discuss trade problems. The most important issue is imported agricultural products. Almost half of the countries attending the conference are protesting pressure to open their markets to foreign farm products, especially beef. Don't expect to see foreign steaks, roast beef, and hamburgers here anytime soon. Little progress is expected. The issue of beef is important for the protesting countries, since several leaders are facing elections this year. Farmers are demanding protection. This is Sarah Flint in Paris.

ANCHOR: And if things aren't already crazy enough in San Francisco, rock star Jerry Ward announced today that he is entering the race for mayor. Ward is best known for his loud music and his pink hair. He hopes to use his popularity and his well-known support of striking hospital workers to make up for his late start. Ward was active in the strike at city hospitals last year when he appeared with several hundred doctors, nurses, and other medical workers at a large rally. Ward knows he has to make up for his late start in the election. He says he knows what the people want, because rock is the music of the people. His campaign slogan is: "From the concert hall to City Hall, Jerry's with you." Will the people of San Francisco agree? We'll know in six months. That's when the election will be held.

In sports, the Vancouver Bulldogs beat the Portland Wildcats eleven to one. The eleven-to-one win was pitcher Juan Sanchez's second win of the season. Don Bryce pitched for the Wildcats. The Bulldogs are the only team with no losses this season. Can they remain undefeated? We'll find out when they play the San José Lions tomorrow. That game will be played in San José. The Bulldogs-Lions game will be broadcast live at seven o'clock tomorrow night.

And finally, from New York. Passengers on Transglobal Airlines flight sixty-five were in for a surprise yesterday. Flight sixty-five was waiting to take off at New York's Kennedy Airport when passengers heard a loud banging on the plane's door. When the crew checked, they found the plane's pilot. He had been locked out. The plane took off ten minutes late.

That's the news. Have a good evening. [*music*]

Unit 20 Dreams and screams

Page 64, Listening Task 1: That's strange.

Listen to two stories about unusual creatures. Write three or more facts about each story.

NUMBER 1: Space creatures

[*Music*]

FIRST STORYTELLER: Many people say that they have seen flying saucers or UFOs – unidentified flying objects. The creatures riding in these UFOs are often described in very similar ways. People say that visitors from space are short – about one hundred twenty-five centimeters, or four feet tall. Their heads are large and they have no hair. Their eyes and mouths are very big too. In fact, their large eyes and mouths make their faces look something like frogs. Some people who have seen them say extraterrestrials are green, but others are not so sure. They don't know what color they are. Most of us get our ideas of space creatures from movies. In fact, the aliens in some movies do look very similar to what people say they have seen. Did people really see these creatures? Or did they see the movies first and then imagine they saw visitors from outer space?

NUMBER 2: The Loch Ness monster

SECOND STORYTELLER: Loch Ness is the largest lake in Scotland. It's a very deep and cold lake. For hundreds of years, people have talked about a monster which lives in the lake. About seventy years ago, a new road was built near the lake. Two people driving down the road saw something moving in the lake. It was Nessie, the Loch Ness monster. They said that the animal was playing, rolling around in the water. Since then, many people say they have seen the monster. Their descriptions are always the same. It looks like a dinosaur, with a very long neck and small head. It has a big bump on its back. People have tried to photograph the animal, but the pictures have not been very clear. Scientists don't know whether there really is a monster or not. Some say it may be a whale or a very large fish. Others think it's a snake. Others say there's nothing at all. Maybe we'll never know what's in Loch Ness.

Do you think UFOs and space creatures are real? Do you believe in the Loch Ness monster?

Page 65, Listening Task 2: Wait until the master comes.

Look at the words and pictures. What do you think the story is about? Listen to the story.

THIRD STORYTELLER: One day an old man went for a walk in the woods. He lost his way and it began to get dark, so he looked around for a place to spend the night. By and by, he came to an old house. He knocked on the door [*knocks on door*] but no one answered. He looked through the window. No one was home. He tried the door. [*door squeaks; opens*] It was open, so he walked in. [*footsteps*]

By now, it was starting to rain. [*sound of rain falling*] There was thunder and lightning. [*loud crack of thunder*] The house was dark and cold, so he decided to make a fire. He looked around, but there was no firewood. There were some old wooden boxes, so he broke them up and made a fire. [*sound of wood cracking*] When he had the fire going a while, he lay down and went to sleep in front of the fireplace.

He had been sleeping only a few minutes when he heard something. [*cat meows*] He woke up. A cat had come into the room. The cat seemed friendly. The man went back to sleep.

When he woke up again, there was a second cat in the room. This cat was bigger than the first one. In fact, it was as big as a wolf. It was looking right at the old man. Soon, it looked at the first cat.

"Shall we do it now?" asked the larger cat.

"No, not now," said the other cat. "Let us wait until the master comes."

The old man thought he was dreaming. He was very tired, so he dropped back to sleep. When he woke up again, there was a third cat in the room. This new cat was as big as a tiger. It looked at the old man. The larger cat asked, "Shall we do it now?" [*cat meows*]

"No," said the others, "let us wait until the master comes."

Soon another cat appeared. It was even larger than the others. Its eyes glowed and its teeth were sharp as knives. It, too, asked, "Shall we do it – now?"

The others said, "No. Let us wait until the master comes." So the largest cat sat down in front of the door.

After a time, it looked at the old man. The look was evil. The largest cat whispered to the others, "It is almost time. The master will be here soon."

At that, the old man jumped up and ran to the window. He jumped out of the window and ran. He ran as fast as he could. He finally stopped. He thought, "At last [*sighs*] I'm safe." [*cat meows*]

Did you like this story? [*pause*] Was it scary?

ACTIVATION

A Listening and Speaking Game

Activation is a review game. The questions and tasks are designed to encourage students to use the forms, functions, and topics they've heard throughout *Active Listening*.

1. Divide the class into groups of three or four. T: *Work in groups of _____ .*

2. Hold your book so that students can see the game on pages 68 and 69. T: *Each group uses one book. Open the book to pages 68 and 69. Put the book on the table.*

3. T: *Each person needs a place marker–a coin, an eraser, or any small object. Put the marker on the "Start here" square.*

4. Point to the "How many spaces?" box on page 69. T: *One person, close your eyes. Touch the "How many spaces?" box with a pencil.*

5. T: *Move that many spaces. Read the sentence or sentences. Answer with at least three things.*

6. T: *Now each partner asks one question about what the first player said.*

7. T: *Continue playing. Take turns.*

8. Allow students to play for two or three minutes so that they understand the game. Then introduce the information about "Teamwork" spaces. T: *When you land on a "Teamwork" space, everyone answers. The next time someone lands on that space, anyone can ask that person a question.*

9. Allow adequate time for students to play.

NOTES

• Although *Activation* reviews language from the entire syllabus, you may wish to have students play it before they have finished the book.

• With activities that have several steps, sometimes giving instructions is difficult, particularly in large classes. It is usually better to demonstrate. Divide the class into groups. Direct one group through the game as one member from each of the other groups watches. Those members then return to their own groups and teach the other players what to do.

• Many students enjoy playing the game more than once. If they change partners each time they play, the information will remain new.

• If there is a question someone doesn't want to answer, allow any other player to ask a different question.

• *Activation* is best used as a cooperative game. It is not necessary to give points. However, if you feel your students need the extra support of competition, you can give points for each sentence a student says while answering each item.

• Because this is a fluency game, corrections are usually not appropriate while the students play.